THE
ORACLE

UNIVERSAL

LAW OF PROSPERITY

DEFYING

ALL

OTHERS

AARON BROWN

WESTBOW
PRESS®
A DIVISION OF THOMAS NELSON
& ZONDERVAN

This book is a work of non-fiction. Unless otherwise noted, the author and the publisher
make no explicit guarantees as to the accuracy of the information contained in this book
and in some cases, names of people and places have been altered to protect their privacy.

WestBow Press books may be ordered through booksellers or by contacting:

WestBow Press
A Division of Thomas Nelson & Zondervan
1663 Liberty Drive
Bloomington, IN 47403
www.westbowpress.com
1 (866) 928-1240

Because of the dynamic nature of the Internet, any web addresses or links contained in
this book may have changed since publication and may no longer be valid. The views
expressed in this work are solely those of the author and do not necessarily reflect the
views of the publisher, and the publisher hereby disclaims any responsibility for them.

Any people depicted in stock imagery provided by Thinkstock are models,
and such images are being used for illustrative purposes only.
Certain stock imagery © Thinkstock.

Scripture quotations marked (NIV) are taken from the Holy Bible, New International
Version®, NIV®. Copyright © 1973, 1978, 1984, 2011 by Biblica, Inc.™ Used
by permission of Zondervan. All rights reserved worldwide. www.zondervan.
com The "NIV" and "New International Version" are trademarks registered
in the United States Patent and Trademark Office by Biblica, Inc.™

Scripture taken from the New King James Version®. Copyright © 1982
by Thomas Nelson. Used by permission. All rights reserved.

Taken from The Call by Os Guinness (c) 1998 by Word. Used by
permission of Thomas Nelson. www.thomasnelson.com.

ISBN: 978-1-5127-4691-4 (sc)
ISBN: 978-1-5127-4692-1 (hc)
ISBN: 978-1-5127-4690-7 (e)

Library of Congress Control Number: 2016910102

Print information available on the last page.

WestBow Press rev. date: 09/19/2019

CONTENTS

PREFACE

Universal principles permeate this world. Fashioned by a grand designer, they waver not, for what God says, is so. Period. Truth is absolute and stubbornly unyielding, even if the whole of humanity were to deny it. A wealth of prophecies circulate and surround us offering wisdom, guidance, and hope. But one prophecy stands alone from all others in significance and scope, and the fate of an individual will hinge upon his response to it. With astonishing life-altering potential, this single principle boasts promises almost too good to be true. Almost.

The Oracle is indeed radical. Enduring as the foremost prophecy in existence and lurking long before ever inscribed, its claims stand unparalleled and unprecedented. The promises declared are as sound and readily available today as in ancient times when initially penned.

The Oracle is profound, ensuring the transformation of life and soul to the one who observes its premise. Remaining unbelievably simple in concept, few will take notice and heed its call despite assurances to quench our innermost longings.

The Oracle is universal and firmly established, though few have recognized the magnitude and tested its bold claims. The prophecies herein are alive and powerful, and ready to act in favor of the one who commits to its philosophy. Sadly, the core precepts remain grossly unchallenged.

The intention of this book is by no means an exhaustive study, for certainly volumes could be written upon each chapter. Verses have been selected and singled out from their original context. I encourage the reader to go to the source and read them in the setting from which they were borrowed for both deeper conviction and further enlightenment. If at some point, the reader may deem the subject matter at all redundant, it is merely because it follows a similar recurrence throughout the Scriptures as each assured blessing is addressed. God's motives for repetition in teaching us the path to prosperity are primarily two-fold, and anything but subtle. Firstly, no other principle comes close in prominence. All other standards, morals, and beliefs arise from the sole premise of the Oracle. Secondly, God knows we are extremely stubborn and willful creatures, necessitating continual prodding.

If the source and origins of the Oracle stem from the mind of man, its precepts are undoubtedly debatable and suspect. If the source is God, however, the debate is moot. A myriad of biblical verses will be noted and used to support the premise for this book. The Scriptures claim inerrancy, inspiration by God, and thus its contents should be trusted as such. To the person who treats select Scriptures as true and valid, while dismissing others as unreliable or false, I submit the entire Word of God stands on shaky ground, and will be entrusted only to the degree it aligns with the preferences and liking of that individual. The whole of Scripture is undependable to that soul and its wisdom and guidance altered toward the fancy of the reader. What is one to believe but that which one reckons believable? One must trust all of Scripture, or else toss it out completely on the basis of it being tainted and untrustworthy.

A popular idea exists presently whereby the power to transform one's destiny to heights of fruition stems from within each soul. What a person focuses his mind upon will determine the course of his fate, as he coerces the world into gifting his every whim. Positive thinking, the law of attraction, and the power of self may induce whatever you want the world to render you.

Considering the air of truth that a confident and proactive individual is better apt to generate his desires into reality, the universe by no means obeys the demands of its creatures. If so, that would manifest each being as god, and personify said universe a living entity with no recourse but submission to the will of all man-exalted gods. While that may sound altogether fascinating and hope-inspiring, it simply is not true. *No, the secret lies elsewhere.*

The truths revealed will undoubtedly be mocked by countless people. While this is no shock, but rather expected, even predicted, this contempt poses no threat and matters little. Indeed, the totality of all scorn is inconsequential, for the premise of the Oracle endures regardless, just as the earth continues its abode long after we have departed. This depicts a far from perfect analogy, for as surely as the earth will one day be no more, the Oracle shall certainly live on.

While some scoff at the Oracle, others will cheerfully agree with its principles, briefly observe them, and shortly fall away from lack of faith and commitment. The majority will be easily distracted by the cares of this world and the illusions it boasts. Unfortunately, the mirage of this life is all too real for many to dismiss. And yet, I suppose if a person budges from point A to B or from point K to L in one's life-long pursuit of God, perhaps all shall not be in vain.

But a few, a scant few, I dare say, will pursue God passionately. They will observe the Oracle faithfully. They will fear God and love him for whom he is and not for what they might gain. In these God shall take notice, and pouring upon them his boundless favor and goodness, he will award the treasures of life.

If you hold but one thing dear in this life, may it be this. Defend the Oracle with all facets of your being. Guard it with every faculty you possess. Observe the Oracle relentlessly.

Mystery Unveiled

For this commandment which I command you today
is not too mysterious for you, nor is it far off.
It is not in heaven, that you should say,
"Who will ascend into heaven for us and bring it to us,
that we may hear it and do it?"
Nor is it beyond the sea, that you should say,
"Who will go over the sea for us and bring it to us,
that we may hear it and do it?"
But the word is very near you, in your mouth
and in your heart, that you may do it.
See, I have set before you today life and good,
death and evil ...
I have set before you life and death,
blessing and cursing; therefore choose life.
—Deuteronomy 30:11—15, 19 NKJV

The Promise Of Prosperity

Imagine for a moment there existed a universal principle claiming origins beyond this worldly realm, touting prosperity to any who observed its elementary doctrine. What would this knowledge be worth? Who would pursue its path, regardless of inevitable cynics teeming all around?

As portrayed in a famed parable, envision you are strolling across a field and suddenly discover a vast fortune buried beneath the ground. What would you do? You would likely drop everything to acquire that piece of property. Your full attention now focused upon your new discovery, you would hurdle any obstacle impeding your way. If necessary, you would undoubtedly sell all your possessions in order to purchase the esteemed plot.

The Oracle offers much more than hidden treasure to anyone who understands its mystery and then determines to follow its course. If pursued, the Oracle is capable of richly fulfilling every facet of one's being, promising not only abundance but good health, security and protection, peace, hope, purpose, and joy. Nothing less than a completely satisfied life and well-being are fruits for the one who devotes his or her life toward observing the Oracle.

The Oracle promises prosperity!

I realize the negative connotation the word *prosperity* may presently summon, as misguided messages abound that seek to charm the naive, so bear with me as we delve further.

THE ORACLE IS TIMELESS

The Oracle originated before time began. It has always been and forever will be; its source has no beginning and shall have no end. The Oracle is a constant and is unchanging. From ancient scriptures, the prophecy reveals the secret to this life and promises prosperity to any who embrace its message. Inseparably coexisting through time, it reveals a universal, cardinal law. It matters not whether man acknowledges its significance, nor if he believes in its precepts. Even if the entire world scorns its principles, the Oracle stands firm on its own accord.

Humans are finite, created and born along a particular moment in a precise place. Conversely, God and the Oracle are infinite—neither born nor created. They are as alive and true today as before the spinning of the sphere in which we live.

The Oracle was conveyed upon the earth since its conception. Exemplified through the Tree of Knowledge of Good and Evil, the

Oracle reinforces the belief of a sovereign Creator who remains in charge over creation. Anything to the contrary is irrational and self-absorbed.

The Oracle Is Universal

The Oracle was extended to Adam and Eve in the Garden of Eden. Fashioned with excellence, they enjoyed the blessings and well-being from this standard of God until they veered and followed the dictates of their hearts. Life changed dramatically for the pair and curses upon them fell.

Yet one will find the Oracle pleasantly merciful to the man who seeks to remedy his wrongful behavior. Fortunately, the Oracle is extremely forgiving to the contrite spirit who genuinely longs to be faithful.

Throughout the ages, the Oracle has been available to everyone. It is obtainable by you and me. Unprejudiced, it will not take sides and holds no biases. Prosperity rests in anticipation for the one who longs to succeed, for the thirsty soul who yearns for the rewards it ensures. It lingers in the shadows for the one willing to sacrifice for a greater cause, ready to embrace the most radical principle in the world, and eager to adopt a transformation of thought and perspective.

Tragically, few trust in its teachings and are even more reluctant to delve into any type of sacrifice. There lies the irony, for the profit in surrendering immorality far outweighs the necessary forfeit—not to mention those things ought to be foregone anyway!

What Is The Oracle?

To satisfy our purposes, an oracle in the broad sense is "a divine communication or revelation."[1] It represents a clear directive from God to man.

More exclusively, the specific Oracle we shall focus upon

is found in the ancient scriptures, from Genesis to Revelation. Inescapably and inseparably woven throughout both Old and New Testaments, it boasts a central theme. Even deprived of these, its petition is practically penned upon our personal hearts and conscience. *The Oracle is the bold prophecy proclaiming prosperity to anyone who fears the Lord God*, Creator of this world and the laws of the universe contained within.

The volume of verses regarding a life prospering by way of obedience is staggering. And while the concept is simple in theory, few have grasped the absolute importance of such a concept, nor have they understood its legitimate presence. It remains too religious or outlandish to allow a complete commitment. And thus, the philosophy prevails untried and untested, and for lack of realized benefit, it is swept from the psyche as quickly as it appears.

People love formulas. If I perform *a* plus *b* plus *c*, I will inevitably get *d*. Or, if I cut out five hundred calories per day and run thirty minutes three times per week, I will lose three pounds in a week—guaranteed. We want to know exactly what we need to do in order to attain viable and reliable results. The Oracle, in contrast, is by no means a formula, yet it bears a general principle showering prosperity upon the observer. God may rightfully bless in any manner he elects, and if he decides to withhold blessing for any length of time, until even the life thereafter, he has all authority to do so as well.

The author of the Oracle's philosophy is God, and he may be neither confined to a box nor reduced to a formula. God desires in us more than mere ritual or formality in action to receive his blessings. *He wants our hearts*. Therefore, observing the Oracle begins in the soul—or the mind. Whether readily apparent or not, we are each faced with a monumental decision. An individual either places himself upon the throne of his life, living as he deems, or he humbly submits to the will of God. He chooses to please himself or rather sacrifices his own prerogative to please God. When once the choice is made to pursue the path of God, a paradigm shift in his mind has begun. That is not to imply that he will follow after him flawlessly, but a radical change in his perspective should result in a drastic alteration of behavior.

The foundation for the Oracle is remarkably straightforward. *If we fear God, we will dwell in prosperity.* Conceived by the Creator himself, we are to conform to this universal law and the guidelines set forth to ensure his presence and favor in our lives. Incorporating a code of ethics, or a manner of living, it promises success and fulfillment in life. Nevertheless, the Oracle prevails a secret to the masses, though the whole of Scripture proclaims its message. It remains a mystery even to those who trust in the idea but are unwilling to devote themselves to the call. Perhaps no other extraordinary prophecy lingers so obscurely from the public eye, presently lost beneath layers of dust atop countless Bibles everywhere!

I hear what some of you are thinking. The Oracle sounds like a *prosperity message.* So allow me to clarify for a moment, if I may, to pacify any potential misunderstanding. The Oracle most certainly *is* a prosperity message! For this I render neither apology nor cower in shame or self-reproof. There is nothing wrong or unethical with a message promoting success in life, *as long as its source is legitimately authorized by God and not taken out of context for thwarted intent.* Otherwise, we are reduced to tossing the Bible from our midst, for its principal message from beginning to end comprises one of prosperity.

Will critics surface? Naturally, for as long as two individuals inhabit the earth, an objector will emerge. God himself has drawn innumerable. If none appear, severe grounds for concern are employed, for either nothing I state is significant and worthy of criticism, or I exist alone in the world void of human interaction. Or worse yet, I am institutionalized for having gone mad, oblivious to any opposition at all. But I propose that even then I would serve my own critic to lash out upon myself, for such is the quibbling nature of humanity.

To clarify, the message of prosperity I refer to is *God inspired* and stands in brave opposition to man-induced prosperity messages.

INSPIRED BY GOD

The apostle Paul delivers a clear warning to us all: "Do not despise prophecies" (1 Thess. 5:20). When God conveys an instruction to follow, we must assume special care to both listen and heed his directive. The commands of God are to be read and observed with utmost gravity.

To be deemed reliable and trustworthy, one must consider whether the message is simply reasoned and justified by man, full of hype and false hope, or else God inspired. There does exist a danger, too, as with any sound, biblical teaching, in borrowing select scriptures and inadvertently basing one's life around them with little regard for the rest of God's Word. One must be mindful of both context and manner in which each biblical theme is entwined with the purpose of God, or a misguided message and intent may suffer. This may well offer a partial explanation for literally tens of thousands of denominations arising from one incarnated immortal Being. For this reason, a plethora of scriptures have been woven herein to shed light of congruence upon a main theme throughout the Word of God, specifically, God's desire to forgive and bless every man and woman who humbly submits to his sovereignty.

It was not until man turned from God that the manner of prosperity was both burdened and hindered. Everything changed that day. A pure world became clouded and contaminated with the odors of sin and offense, and man was driven from the garden. A holy God will not, and I submit, *cannot* allow impurity to persist without consequence, or holy he no longer will be.

So while the Oracle unveils the path to prosperity, it likewise bears a curse to all who neglect or violate its precepts. The world as we know it is filled with complications, sickness, confusion, anxiety, and a glut of other accursed effects. But hope is ignited with those who heed the Oracle's charge and actively pursue it. God desires to restore the havoc running rampant throughout the world and within each member's life. Not only is he willing, but God actively wishes to reverse the misfortunes of the curse and rain down upon man his restoration.

The promises of God are true, but beware of the inclination to gravitate toward a polar extreme with little regard. To venture away from the power and validity of his promises is to water down the very words of God. On the other hand, demanding the rewards professed loses sight of God's grand canvas of life and boasts an obedience met by one's personal standard. A common tendency is to drift toward the center, aligning perfectly between each opposing pole and finding a comfortable complacency to hold God's promises to a pinnacle of lukewarmness. So where should one abide but in the confidence that his words are to be trusted and pursued, while leaving the outcome in the hands of God and according to his sovereign plan.

Blessings and curses are often tied to obedience and faithfulness toward God's rules, demonstrating our fear of God or lack thereof. One of the beautiful things about the Oracle is its compassion, in that, regardless of past behavior of how poorly one has tread the earth, present and future adherence to its counsel may very well alter the fate of an individual's life course. The mercies of God are new *every* morning. When one turns from his immoral ways to pursue the Oracle, the compass of his life is realigned according to the goodness and purposes of God.

Do you wish to know true fulfillment in this world? Do you desire a genuine personal joy so difficult to grasp and maintain? Do you yearn to fill the void in your soul and gain a deep-seeded peace regardless of current circumstances? Do you long for a blessed and prosperous life now? Fear God. Nothing else will compare. Nothing else has so much to offer. Fear him with love and a thankful heart. Fear him for the compassion and mercies he freely spills over. Fear him from desperation of present situation or troubled conditions. Dare I even suggest, but to the one who may lack the spiritual maturity and perception of our marvelous depravity and poverty for God's graces, fear him from selfish greed if for little else. *But fear God!*

We do well to remember that God's perspective on prosperity is often substantially different from that of the world. Jesus is the epitome of prosperity, if you will, and yet he owned few possessions, was hated by many, and then brutally killed. If the Oracle is observed, though you die or tragedy befalls, know you have pleased God. He smiles upon you and blesses as only he recognizes best how. For what is death anyway but a temporary separation, as the soul continues to endure? You remain just as alive, though the body ceases to function as before. What a sorrowful, yet joyful celebration a funeral ought be for a passing child of God to those of us who also believe!

You will never go wrong if you follow God wholeheartedly and place him above all else. Even if all seems to fail in your life, you are a success in the eyes of God.

THE ONE SOUL

Over seven billion people in the world are alive today. Of those, consider how many billions trust in a god made from human fabrication or multiple gods who fail to exist. The remaining number dwindles sharply. Then subtract those who claim either atheism or no belief whatsoever. Millions and millions have no care in the issue and boast an unshakeable indifference. Now imagine the fraction who are left, those who trust in God, Creator of heaven and earth. From this group, withdraw any who are insincere and enjoy no real relationship with him.

Few remain, if one is honest. Finally, from this company of genuine believers, ponder how many are truly pursuing God and seeking to honor him above self and egocentric ambitions. How many are not only willing, but actually sacrifice their own wills for the sake of the will of God. How many turn from sin, even the secret sins of the heart that no one knows but God himself? How many place God first, unwilling to compromise principles and integrity in order to please the one who gives life?

I submit the number is miniscule. We are not speaking of perfection here, of course, for each person, regardless of commitment to God, will inevitably sin until the day he dies. Adrian Rogers used to explain his involvement with sin before and after his conversion. Prior to knowing God, he would readily run toward sin, as the natural man is inclined. But after becoming a Christian, he still sinned, though now he ran *from* sin. One's desire should shift toward actually wanting to choose obedience.

The Bible teaches that Satan runs to and fro throughout the earth, hunting whom to destroy. He is depicted as running frantically, in haste, to find any he might deceive and draw away from God. He is clever and highly successful in his temporary mission.

God, conversely, is neither running nor frantic, and yet, he is continually looking for one who is faithful. He is searching for the one man, the one woman, who holds him in high regard through obedience. I propose this task is hardly challenging at all for God, as he glances across a dwarf globe in pursuit of an occasional elite light dotting an expanse of utter darkness. But what illumination those tiny specks emit! I imagine the eyes of God immediately drawn to the bold and committed flames that serve his unwavering children. His heart burns for his sons and daughters, and his favor and protection promptly rests upon them.

Noah was a righteous man, faithful to God. By no means perfect, his allegiance caught the attention of God as he spared his life amidst a wicked world. All were evil—except one man! But that was enough to win God's heart. Noah enjoyed the favor of God, even to the point of God sparing his closest family from the flood, while righteous they were not. But one man made a difference.

Though the entire world hedges a wall against God and goes their own way, he seeks the one who will honor him no matter the cost. God will pursue that *one soul* and unleash his boundless goodness and blessing upon him.

The Oracle Is Radical

The Oracle defies the logic and wisdom this world proudly boasts. Only those who invite humility comprehend its significance, while the arrogant and self-sufficient receive its content with disinterest. The precepts of the Oracle are lost in obscurity to most, though its astonishing potential may be unlocked by anyone, anywhere. The precepts of the Oracle are strong and sound, and withstand the masses who continually oppose its message.

The meek hear its call. It yells to no one. Instead, it whispers with such clarity and truth to the one who will stop and listen. It challenges, even dares us to observe and discover whether we are able to contain the blessings that may be poured upon us, if only we heed its instruction.

The Oracle Is Reliable

The bulk of this world is unreliable. Machines wear out and break down. Computers acquire viruses and glitches. Even people, inundated with a sinful nature, hypocrisy, and humanity, will inevitably let you down at some point. Few surprises there. But one thing that remains certain and reliable is the Oracle. The cause and effect relationship surrounding those with or without the fear of the Lord is steadfast and unwavering. Whether positive or negative, a suitable outcome forever trails behavior.

Immoral conduct leads to unfavorable consequences. Though a person may readily agree with this concept, the problem arises where few people associate the specific outcome with the poor choice made. An individual falls into sin, and shortly thereafter, something adverse occurs in his life. Instead of recognizing the cause and effect kinship involved, he complains that life is unfair, for bad things always happen to him. While that may be true, it may also simply be that he continually runs toward a lifestyle of iniquity.

Once a person discovers and internalizes the fear of the Lord in his personal life, the principle nature of the Oracle persists, but it now begins to pivot in the *favor* of the humbled and broken man. It is at this point where he finds real strength through his brokenness to the Lord, and in his weakness he is made strong. No doubt this sounds foolish to society, but that is how God works. His ways are indeed delightfully contrary to those of the world!

- The Oracle is timeless. It has neither beginning nor ending and existed before the origin of time.

- The Oracle is universal. It is offered to any who grasp its understanding and pursue compliance.

- Prosperity is promised to the one who seeks to honor and observe the Oracle, to the soul who fears God.

- The Oracle is a primary theme woven throughout the Word of God. It whispers from the depth of each soul, revealing the very secret to life.

- The Oracle is a general principle, and the blessings received are not always what we expect.

- A radical change in our perspective is imperative in properly observing the Oracle. One must shift from an egocentric will to one of submission to the manner of living God requires.

- Though readily available to everyone, this astounding prophecy remains a mystery to the masses.

- God is seeking the one soul who chooses to honor him, that he might unleash his goodness upon him.

- Once a person internalizes the fear of the Lord in his life, the Oracle begins to pivot in the favor of the humbled and broken man.

THE ORACLE SIMPLIFIED

> An oracle within my heart concerning
> the transgression of the wicked:
> There is no fear of God before his eyes ...
> He has ceased to be wise and to do good.
> —Psalm 36:1, 3

Be not misled. The fear of the Lord has absolutely nothing to do with organized religion, praying, or even reading the Word of God. A man may easily attend church seven days per week and read his Bible three hours each day, and still possess no fear of the Lord. Though outward behaviors generally support and confirm its presence, it has little to do with externalities.

The fear of the Lord is not so much concerned with the physical as it is with the mental and emotional capacities of the soul. What the eye witnesses externally is frequently absent from the spirit, as hypocrisy routinely runs rampant throughout human nature. We observe the outer facade of man while the darker, sinister, more factual side lies latent in the shadows. On the other hand, if one genuinely honors God with his thoughts and spirit, his words and actions will invariably follow.

WHAT IS THE FEAR OF THE LORD?

The fear of the Lord is a matter of the heart. It has much to do with control. Who is in ultimate control of the affairs of man, both individually and corporally? Can we trust in a supreme God to accomplish his perfect and just will, or must we rely on ourselves to intervene and protect our private welfare and interest? The fear of the Lord is an attitude of humility, where we must decide to follow God and voluntarily submit our will over to his. It is internalizing the reality that he is Creator and I am merely his creation.

The fear of God originates when a person grasps an understanding of the presence of God among us, along with the realization of our sinfulness before such a holy Being. The fear of the Lord is sharpened as one comprehends how small and perverse we are compared to God's righteousness. It is knowing we fall so short of his holiness, and recognizing our absolute need of God where only his grace can afford.

Throughout Scripture, a divine presence always induced fear within man. A deeply rooted awe and dread infiltrated each individual who experienced such an encounter. When unholy man meets holy God, fear is the natural and involuntary response. Man is hopeless and utterly vulnerable before a perfect and omnipotent God. Even Saul, immersed in hatred and disdain for God and his people, when confronted by the Lord, fell to the ground in lowliness and terror. Upon perceiving his dire need for God, the pride of Saul was decimated and he transformed into Paul, one of the greatest inspired writers of the Word of God. Pride must be squashed in the soul of man before God may assume control of his life. Only then is he able to actualize and unleash the favor of God.

When man understands his depravity before God, a reverential awe should ensue. After Adam and Eve sinned, they hid from fear and insecurity of their nakedness. And yet, when a person trusts in the grace of God, one gains the assurance he is for us, not against us. Scripture claims he fights on our behalf and will never leave us. What a comfort to rest in the fear of the Lord.

Fear in this regard is not a negative quality at all, but one in which we discover fellowship and camaraderie with the Maker of the world. As one submits to the authority of God, all other fears should melt as one realizes God is in control of the affairs of his life. What harm can mere man possibly commit, except that which God permits in his sovereign and perfect will?

The Israelites departed from the land of Egypt where they served as slaves, and God spoke through Moses. "If you will indeed obey My voice and keep My covenant, then you shall be a special treasure to Me above all people; for all the earth is Mine" (Exod. 19:5). Little has changed. The earth still belongs to God, and whoever obeys God today will be a special treasure to him.

God spoke again to Moses from Mount Sinai amidst lightning, thundering, and smoke wafting from the mountain. The Israelites were terrified. Moses explained to them, "Do not fear; for God has come to test you, and that His fear may be before you, so that you may not sin" (Exod. 20:20). Basically, do not fear, but indeed, be fearful! Their sense of fear was misguided. Do not be afraid of the thunder and lightning, but *do* fear a holy God. An appropriate fear of the holiness of God discourages sinful behavior, while encouraging faithfulness toward such a hallowed Being.

What a wonderfully ironic notion, that as we properly fear the Lord, we are to rejoice with trembling adoration (Ps. 2:11). The world is commanded to tremble and worship God simultaneously (Ps. 96:9). What a joy and comfort to know our God is righteous and omnipotent. I can imagine nothing more frightening than a God who is either immoral or limited in power.

ACTIVELY FEARING GOD

How does a person actively fear God? The Bible lays out the answer clearly again and again, almost to the point of exhaustion, though man stubbornly refuses to abide. We are instructed to walk in the ways of God, while loving and serving him with all our heart.

Proverbs 8:13 reveals, "the fear of the Lord is to hate evil". God hates immorality, so likewise, man ought to hate it. Man must love the things God loves if he is to share a right relationship with him. Man is to be like-minded with his Creator, hating wickedness while pursuing righteousness. Sounds simple.

Unfortunately, a frightening number of Christians demonstrate an admirable faith on Sunday morning, but interest fades once the church door shuts behind them on the way out. Their belief system, while seemingly real amongst the pews, morphs as the physical world assumes a greater role in their lives, snuffing out spiritual awareness. It is a shallow faith they own, living a life wholly opposed to the morals they profess at church. They need God, for sure, to sustain them through difficult times, but a relationship involving obedience and sacrifice is another thing altogether.

Religion is a subtle swindler used by Satan to avert the people of God from an actual relationship with him. Repulsive to God, the foul odor of religion is welcomed with open arms by the devil. The Pharisees were clearly proud of their religiosity and legalistic lifestyle, and yet they were the ones rebuked by Jesus for their self-righteousness and deception. Pharisaical faith was superficial and their love for God a counterfeit.

The fear of the Lord is an attitude toward God, contingent upon the manner in which a person views him. The man lacking remorse or shame for his immorality has yet to understand the fear of the Lord, for it belongs to the repentant soul. To the extent man believes he exists alone in this world apart from the influences of God, he will not understand the fear of the Lord, nor grasp its significance.

THE HOLINESS OF GOD

Jesus instructs the believer to pray, "Our Father in heaven, hallowed be Your name" (Luke 11:2). His name is hallowed, for he is holy. To emphasize this absolute quality, the Bible portrays the Lord as holy, holy, holy. Scripture stresses no other characteristic of God three times except when describing his holiness. The moment a man recognizes his depravity before such a holy Being, he should feel a genuine sense of terror and awe. Throughout the Bible, when a person found himself in the presence of the divine, he immediately fell to the ground in fear and reverence. A proper sense of unworthiness instinctively flooded his soul.

Few things tangible are truly holy upon earth. The Holy Spirit, though his presence felt, exists unseen in this world. The Father remains involved in the affairs of man, and may listen and respond to his petitions, but he remains veiled from our sight nonetheless. I can think of a single tangible element alone in this world which may boast a holy status: the Word of God.

Inspired by God through man, the original text was penned flawless and faultless. How peculiar, how intriguing, this holy Bible, we may touch with human hands and see with physical eyes. Surviving thousands of years in accuracy, amidst countless attempts of eradication and efforts toward banishment, the Bible continues to transform lives. Its worth can be compared to no other book, nor any other thing for that matter, but may be obtained for so little. Why, copies are dispersed without any charge at all! And yet, who cares? We have grown numb to its message, its purpose, and its holiness.

When at last a man recognizes his sinful state before a supremely divine Being, an appropriate fear of God should emanate. The man is at once exposed, weak, humbled, and unsafe amidst such holiness. His spirit has been challenged and convicted, and found infinitely lacking on its own.

FREE WILL

What a terrific privilege we possess for free will. God graciously gives us the choice to either love or reject him. He will not force us one way or the other. It reminds me of a line from the movie Bruce Almighty, where Jim Carey is granted the opportunity to be God for one day. Upon accepting the challenge, he finds himself frustrated by the complexity in getting a person to love him. Jim articulates an insightful question to Morgan Freeman, who plays the true God in the film. "How do you make someone love you without affecting free will?"[2]

Though not a theologically accurate movie script in the least, it poses a thought-provoking question worth pondering. While God does draw a person toward himself, each individual has the responsibility to respond to his call, whether to love God or else deny him. God will not force a proper decision.

Solomon offers an interesting morsel of truth, where "the eyes of the Lord are in every place, keeping watch on the evil and the good" (Prov. 15:3). I say interesting, for it serves both a warning and a source of encouragement, depending upon the reader of the passage. God knows and sees everything, including our actions, words, thoughts, intentions, and motivations behind all we do. What a sobering thought for us all! But how inspiring, at the same time, that God recognizes all the good, with a heart to bless the faithful few.

Who are the faithful? Those who live by faith in the Word of God and follow his commands. The Bible is clear that a person cannot please God without faith. If someone fears God, he will honor him by doing his will. If he chooses disobedience, he lacks the fear of the Lord, at least at some level. I am confident that if we actually heard God tell us to do this or that, we would surely comply. And yet, he *has* instructed us quite distinctly, though not audibly. Thus, enter faith and humility, or else deficiency of faith and egotistical independence.

The Choice

The choice is ours individually. Obey God and discover blessing, or else turn from God and be cursed. It is truly that simple.

But first, what exactly are blessings and curses? We can think of a blessing as "the invoking of God's favor upon a person" or "a favor or gift bestowed by God, thereby bringing happiness."[3] A curse may be defined as the cause of misfortune, trouble, or doom to befall a person or group.[4]

> Behold, I set before you today a blessing and a curse:
> the blessing, if you obey the commandments of the Lord...
> and the curse, if you do not obey the commandments
> of the Lord your God, but turn aside
> from the way which I command you.
> —Deuteronomy 11:26—28

This promise is repeated so often throughout Scripture, the earnest reader will find the message impossible to ignore. To dismiss the appeal, the student would need to disregard the entire Word of God, for the warning is so entwined from beginning to end.

We can believe this by faith, choose to follow God, and receive his blessings. Otherwise, we can doubt the veracity of this prophecy and go our own way. God dispenses blessings and curses according to our actions. The naive confidently bolt ahead, "There will be no consequence for my deeds," and yet Paul warns us to "not be deceived ... for whatever a man sows, that he will also reap" (Gal. 6:7).

Another boldly blurts, "But I don't believe in God." This conviction is irrelevant. Erroneous beliefs in no way discount the reality that God exists. Be not mistaken, the truth remains true whether or not it is approved or acknowledged by man. One may claim the concept of gravity is fictitious since he is incapable of seeing it, yet when he leaps from a cliff, his flawed belief is immaterial. The consequence proves gravity exists. Faith often stems from experience, not sight.

Still another assures himself, "I only believe in certain portions of Scripture." A conviction of this nature is unreasonable and irrational. Either trust in the whole of Scripture or else none of it. One may not assume the luxury of selecting elements he favors and dismissing the rest. It is God's Book. He will not allow man to determine which parts are welcome and which are unsuitable.

Our behavior continually produces consequences affecting our lives and those around us. If you think about it, the totality of life is the summation of our conduct and the outcomes they yield. It is readily obvious that our actions are extremely significant in determining our future course.

Obedience yields genuine peace, unlike the shallow peace we muster from worldly sources that dissipates as quickly as it appears. Sin, on the other hand, employs slavery to the one who grants its cunning control. Either way, the choice dangles before every person, and whatever is chosen will begin to own that person. One might be led to believe the other way around, but that is the subtle danger of sin. In the beginning, the individual is allotted much power over the trespass. If unrestrained, he slowly and casually relinquishes his power over the alluring infraction, until at once the sin unwittingly assumes control and silently possesses the sinner. The sin is now commonplace, and personal responsibility is reduced and brushed aside as bad habit or addiction.

Secret Of The Lord

The Bible tells us, "the fear of the Lord is the beginning of wisdom; a good understanding have all those who do His commandments" (Ps. 111:10). According to this scripture and others similar, the fear of the Lord is the very *foundation* of wisdom. A person may boast a wealth of intelligence, cleverness, talent, knowledge, and even genius. He may possess book smarts, street smarts, and receive degrees in abundance, yet still lack wisdom. A wise man is inconceivable to the one lacking the fear of the Lord, for the fountain of wisdom has yet to be tasted.

The secret of the Lord is with those who fear Him.
—Psalm 25:14

God enlightens the one who seeks to know him, while a spiritual veil clouds the understanding of the person who rejects God or is merely disinterested. The soul who fears God begins a comprehension of the things of God that are simply unfathomable to the unbeliever.

Consider the most paramount commandment of all. In the words of Jesus, the chief instruction that we could follow is this:

And you shall love the Lord your God with all your heart,
with all your soul, with all your mind,
and with all your strength.
And the second, like it, is this:
"You shall love your neighbor as yourself."
There is no other commandment greater than these.
—Mark 12:30, 31

ACQUIRE THE FEAR OF THE LORD

Those of us who are parents attempt to instill a healthy sense of fear in our children toward us. Do we wish for them to dread or be frightened of us? Of course not, but rather that they might avoid negative consequences that result from poor behavioral choices. Instead, we hope they choose wisely to experience our approval and potential reward.

I have grown weary of formulas for everything these days. Learn in twenty days how to receive answers to prayer. Ten simple steps for losing weight. Six steps to becoming a man of God. While these methods may serve as aids, they are not always necessary and have a way of complicating the real issue.

We could easily conjure up seven steps in fearing the Lord more effectively. But the primary need is faith, and with faith, follow love and humility. They are complementary and should form a stronger bond simultaneously. As the believer more fully comprehends the grace of God, he will grow in humility and love. Scripture tells us we are to love God with all of our heart, mind, soul, and strength, with every facet of our being. Reading further, we learn we show our love for God through obedience to his ways. The principle of the Oracle and the fear of the Lord are so intertwined with this chief commandment, it is undeniably inseparable. If we love God, we will honor him with obedience.

If we believe the promises and warnings of God, our habits should heed his call. It requires faith to live by these beliefs, to be certain, and the degree of faithfulness we display regarding the morality God demands, generally coincides with the level of faith to which we adhere. As faith increases, the maturity of the believer grows.

The fear of the Lord is often misconstrued. While honoring God with a reverential fear, it is at the same time one of the most liberating concepts to the one who embraces its doctrine. *God is terrifyingly wonderful!* Exalting God as the almighty is comforting as one rests in his presence and stability. God is unchanging and constant, and his truths and promises endure regardless of world events or personal situation. He is a rock, unmoving and in complete control at all times.

It matters little what man says or thinks relative to God. Peer pressures dissipate as one lives to please him. We are strengthened to stand strong amidst a world of selfish gain, and free to live as the one who created us intended. As one further comprehends and adopts the fear of the Lord for himself, a *release* of fear is discovered as one channels his anxieties and concerns upon the shoulders of God.

One may argue that love and fear should not endure together. While the two emotions may very well coexist, it is not an unhealthy argument entirely. For if a person loves God as he ought, he would obey his commands, and thereby, exempt himself from any fear of discipline that may otherwise unfold. The faithful servant can live in the confidence that God is for him. When a person understands the love God sheds for him, he possesses a wholesome fear driven by love instead of terror. As a believer places God at the helm of his life, yielding his allegiance to him alone, all other fears and worries are allowed to fade.

The fear of the Lord has been all but lost in our society. Even among Christian circles, people are desensitized to the concept. They have grown indifferent to the holiness of God and to the godly lifestyle required. If grace forgives and cleanses from all sin, which indeed it does, then living above reproach is forfeited for the sake of pleasures to be forgiven. The believer lives a life indistinguishable from the unbeliever as he offensively embraces the penalty paid for him upon the cross.

- An appropriate fear of God should arise when a person becomes aware of God's presence, and recognizes his depravity before a perfectly holy, supreme Being.

- The fear of the Lord is sharpened as one comprehends how small and perverse we are compared to the righteousness of God.

- As we submit to God's authority, all other fears should dissipate as we realize God is in control of the affairs in our life.

- A proper fear of the holiness of God discourages sinful behavior.

- Every individual is faced with a choice. Obey God and be blessed, or turn from God and be cursed.

- We actively fear the Lord by loving him and walking in his ways.

- The principle of the Oracle is inseparable from the greatest commandment of all, to love God with all of our heart.

- The soul who fears the Lord begins a comprehension of God unfathomable to the unbeliever.

- Our behavior produces consequences affecting our lives and those around us. Our life is the summation of our conduct and the outcomes they yield.

WHY FEAR GOD?

Do not fear those who kill the body
but cannot kill the soul.
But rather fear Him who is able to destroy
both soul and body in hell.
—Matthew 10:28

THE SIN OF PRIDE

Man, as a whole, has all but forgotten God. It is a new age—the age of self. We have an inherent right to behave as we please, to purchase what we want without possessing the money, and to believe what we wish, as long as it fits our personal world opinion. Man is entitled to acquire anything pleasurable or beneficial through the laws of positive thinking and attraction. The universe must listen to me and grant whatever I ask of it.

The principal problem here is replacing the control and authority of God with the egotism of man. This is none other than the sin of pride, and is precisely the cause of the rebellion and fall of the angel Lucifer. Sin is seating oneself on the throne of his life, and disregarding the authority of God. Os Guinness offers insight regarding the reversed mentality of the contemporary man. "Professing to be unsure of God, they pretend to be sure of themselves. Followers of Christ put things the other way around: Unsure of ourselves, we are sure of God."[5]

Upon exploring a few of the reasons we ought to fear God, it seems irrational why anyone would not.

The Authority Of God

This world is wrought with countless fears. We worry about job security, financial loss, and the welfare of our loved ones. We fret over health risks, school performance, and peer pressures. Enemies lurk, criminals prowl, and snakes and spiders bite. Life itself is laced with perils virtually inescapable and unavoidable. We live restlessly about tomorrow, for who knows the trials it may bring? Even the media thrives on drowning its audience with panic and apprehension.

We are anxious creatures, but we need not be. Threats certainly roam in this world worthy of our caution, while other dangers require discernment and common sense to avoid. But beyond this, we must learn to trust God, if he is indeed our God. As King Hezekiah prayed to his Lord thousands of years ago, "You are God, You alone, of all the kingdoms of the earth. You have made heaven and earth" (2 Kings 19:15). Who are we to discount God and trust instead in our own effort and strength?

We must learn to fear God, not man. Though the aggregate of humanity gathered against us, yet God stood firmly aside us, there is no concern. The apostle Paul confirms this in Romans 8:31: "If God is for us, who can be against us?" Genesis recalls a day when millions of people dwelt in opposition to God. The intent of man was continually wicked, so much so that God was actually sorry he made man. What a sobering thought.

But there lived one man who walked with God. *One* man! Noah pleased God. That was enough to find grace and favor in the eyes of God. A single soul. God is not so much concerned with numbers, as he is with the righteous character and faithful hearts of a few. Though he wishes for none to perish, God will never compromise his holiness to tolerate rebellion.

God wants to abide in man, this extraordinarily unique creature he purposefully chose to design in his own likeness. A monumental problem, unfortunately, prevents this presence from occurring. I dare say, the quandary literally *forbids* the indwelling from taking place! For it is impossible for a holy spirit to fill the soul of a man voluntarily living in habitual sin. The very idea violates the character of a Being entirely foreign of sin.

God is the ultimate authority. Everything that exists owes its origin to God. "For every beast of the forest is Mine, and the cattle on a thousand hills. I know all the birds of the mountains, and the wild beasts of the field are Mine" (Ps. 50:10—12). We breathe because he lends us breath. Apart from him, we can do absolutely nothing. By his grace and patience we are not only tolerated, but loved. Why God loves us so much is beyond me, but I praise him for so doing!

Amidst heavy turmoil, Job came to understand the power of God well: "Whatever His soul desires, that He does. For He performs what is appointed for me, and many such things are with Him. Therefore I am terrified at His presence; when I consider this, I am afraid of Him" (Job 23:13—15). Job learned the fear of the Lord, summoning a very present terror, and at the same time, extending surpassing comfort as one basks beneath his complete control.

Amazingly, not only are we to fear the Lord, but inanimate objects and even the laws of physics are subject to the rule of God. "Tremble, O earth, at the presence of the Lord" (Ps. 114:7).

I love the chronicle of the disciples crossing the Sea of Galilee with Jesus one evening. A violent storm developed, tossing waves over the side of the boat. As the boat began filling, the men found Jesus sound asleep in the stern. Fearing impending death, they awakened him. Jesus stood up and rebuked the wind, demanding it to be calm. The wind promptly obeyed. It wavered not. "Why are you so fearful?" Jesus asked the disciples. "How is it that you have no faith?"

Suddenly, the object of their fear shifted. "And they feared exceedingly, and said to one another, 'Who can this be, that even the wind and the sea obey Him!'" (Mark 4:35—41).

Notice the disciples were afraid and marveled at the sudden obedience of the storm. Initially fearful of the might of the storm, the focus of their dread immediately morphed. With the tempest calmed, they were now afraid of something greater. They feared the Man in the boat with them, for the horrific elements of nature obeyed and honored him. The authority of this Man surpassed anything they had ever known.

THE CHARACTER OF GOD

Few words describe the character of God accurately. Words like amazing, wonderful, incredible, and awesome become practically meaningless due to their association with other niceties. They have become grossly watered down with frivolous repetition. We have all enjoyed an awesome day, eaten an amazing pizza, and witnessed an incredible sunset. To then subject these same words to God leaves a void in his portrayal. Limited words remain, and even if a new one was conceived, it too, I am convinced, would soon be diluted to normalcy.

Thankfully, a remnant of savory words endure to help reveal the personality and nature of God. These absolutes benefit in painting a better understanding of why he is worthy of being feared. He is often referred in the Scriptures as almighty. The Lord himself declared to Abram, "I am Almighty God; walk before Me and be blameless" (Gen. 17:1). Fortunately, I know of no others who may rightfully claim the same.

The Psalms are rich in exposing the morality and virtue of God. "He loves righteousness and justice; the earth is full of the goodness of the Lord" (Ps. 33:5). These two attributes are so closely linked together they are virtually inseparable. "Your righteousness, O God, is to the height of heaven, You who have done great things; O God, who is like You?" (Ps. 71:19).

There is none like God, eternal and infinite. He is faithful, loving, and compassionate, yet righteous and just all the while. The

Lord tells us, "I am the Lord, exercising lovingkindness, judgment, and righteousness in the earth. For in these I delight" (Jer. 9:24).

Still other absolutes of God's personality incorporate his omnipotence, omniscience, and omnipresence. God is all-powerful, all-knowing, and everywhere. Nothing happens without either his approval or allowance.

God Is Holy

Another fundamental quality meriting the fear of the Lord, and briefly touched upon already, is the holiness of God. People insist God is a God of love. He certainly is, for he sent his Son to die for us. But too many individuals lose sight of the fact that God is also perfectly righteous. A being may not be somewhat holy, or almost always holy, or even very, very holy. One is purely, completely, and always holy, or he is not holy at all.

God is perfectly and thoroughly holy, without sin, evil intent, or immoral thought. Because of his holiness, a death is required to regain a relationship and fellowship with God. A penalty must be paid to consequence the wrong. A soul either trusts in the death of Christ, or else he must spiritually die himself and suffer eternal separation from his Maker.

God commands his people in Leviticus 19:1 that they "shall be holy, for I the Lord your God am holy." The intention here is to be set apart, or separated from sin. God desires that we each become Christ-like, turning from immorality and conforming to his character.

> The Lord of hosts, Him you shall hallow;
> Let Him be your fear, and let Him be your dread.
> —Isaiah 8:13

When once we begin to understand the holiness of God, we inevitably start to comprehend the fear of the Lord. This reverential fear of His purity will subsequently lead to obedience and a heart seeking to please him. The Bible claims, "He who has clean hands and a pure heart … shall receive blessing from the Lord" (Ps. 24:4, 5). God is searching for the faithful few who will turn aside from a life of sin.

GOD IS JUDGE

Those who have stood before a judge will quickly recognize the weight of intimidation associated with one who holds authority to pass judgment. How dreadful to fall into the hands of one man with the power to punish or condemn for a wrong committed. Yet as frightful as this may be, it will pale in comparison to the horror the man who has rejected God shall face when he departs to meet his Maker.

But make no mistake, for Scripture is crystal clear with whom ultimate authority rests. We are told God himself is Judge (Psalm 50:6). What a chilling thought to know the hand of God works against those who turn against him and his commands (1 Sam. 12:15).

Jesus offers us both a comfort and warning in the book of Luke. He tells us not to be afraid "of those who kill the body, and after that have no more that they can do." Man can take the life of another man, and yet, only with the allowance of God can he do so. Thankfully, the lasting, eternal reality of man is his spirit. His physical body exists only temporarily upon earth, but his value lies within. "But I will show you whom you should fear," Jesus continues, "Fear Him who, after He has killed, has power to cast into hell; yes, I say to you, fear Him!" (Luke 12:4, 5). Man may inflict minimal affliction here on earth, but God is the ultimate Judge. The discernment of God will profoundly affect both temporal and eternal capacities of each and every soul.

Both criminals hanging on crosses alongside Jesus mocked Christ along with the observing multitude. As time droned on, one of the crooks realized this truly was the Messiah, God in the flesh. The man rebuked and warned the other offender for his persistent blaspheming.

"Do you not even fear God, seeing you are under the same condemnation?" he asked. Recognizing the authority of Jesus to save or cast away a soul, he plead, "Lord, remember me when You come into Your kingdom." Jesus' reply could not have been more comforting: "Assuredly, I say to you, today you will be with Me in Paradise" (Luke 23:40—43).

God offers us chance after chance to come to him in repentance. He offers forgiveness through his Son who died in our place, and he desires restored fellowship, if only we humble ourselves. Nevertheless, once the night of life approaches and we leave this world behind, it shall prove too late for restoration.

But what about now, in this present life? Does God judge us while we endure in this world? Without a doubt, for there are definitely current consequences for our behavior.

Much of the Old Testament chronicles the rebellion of God's chosen people, the Israelites, as well as their subsequent repentance and returning to him. "Do you not fear Me?" asked the Lord. "Will you not tremble at My presence?" They repeatedly disobeyed and rejected God only to reap his wrath upon them.

"This people has a defiant and rebellious heart; they have revolted and departed," God explained. "Your iniquities have turned these things away, and your sins have withheld good from you" (Jer. 5:22—25). But God is wonderfully merciful, and as they returned in genuineness of heart, he relented and began healing them from their suffering.

Who knows the amount of good and blessing we have forfeited because of our immoral deeds, thoughts, and intent? Our lives, no doubt, would look different if we lived for God and according to his ways. It is never too late to return to God and unveil his mercy and favor.

If My people who are called by My name will
humble themselves, and pray and seek My face,
and turn from their wicked ways,
then I will hear from heaven,
and will forgive their sin and heal their land.
—2 Chronicles 7:14

Throughout the whole of Scripture, a central message is revealed to the willing reader. The hungry soul discovers a tapestry interlaced from beginning to end that centers upon the fear of the Lord. In Revelation, John testifies that he sees an angel preaching to all peoples of the earth in the future. It is interesting to note that the angel will speak in a loud voice proclaiming the time of God's judgment upon man is quickly arriving. The angel instructs everyone to worship and "fear God and give glory to Him" (Rev. 14:7). This is his shout of warning to all who will listen.

I find it fascinating how God designed within the creation of this world the very means of cleansing it from wickedness. Genesis describes a canopy of water above the earth, and concurrently, subterranean waters below its surface, that were opened and broken to spring the global flood of water in the days of Noah. Perhaps God instilled this manner of refinement on the second day when he said, "Let there be a firmament in the midst of the waters, and let it divide the waters from the waters" (Gen. 1:6). He providentially recognized the impending necessity.

Now we know God will never again destroy the earth by water. But he foretells of a coming devastation upon wicked men by another means. This time the earth will be destroyed by fire (2 Pet. 3:6). What I find so enthralling is that this judgment was forecast thousands of years ago, without any knowledge of the composition of the earth's core. At well over 10,000 degrees Fahrenheit, the outer core of the earth is a molten, burning liquid, hotter than the surface of the sun! When you consider fault lines, earthquakes, and volcanic activity, the potential for devastation upon the earth by fire suddenly becomes a very real possibility.

God tells us those who fear not his name will become stubble. "The day is coming, burning like an oven ... and the day which is coming shall burn them up" (Mal. 4:1). God must soon judge the souls of men. Fear God and worship him in reverential awe. I submit, this remains the key reason for the very existence of Scripture!

God Is Merciful

Psalm parallels the height of the heavens above the earth with God's mercy toward those who fear him (Ps. 103:11). His compassion knows no bounds with the one who reveres his name and is repentant. Remember, it is one thing to be remorseful regarding immoral behavior, but that is not enough. We are told Judas was remorseful upon turning Jesus over to be arrested and crucified. He then hung himself, sadly lacking the necessary repentance we are called toward.

The reference continues, "As a father pities his children, so the Lord pities those who fear Him" (Ps. 103:13). That is the key here, and the fundamental message of the Oracle. God looks at the heart, and little else. Do we fear God with humble adoration, fall at his feet, and submit our will to his? I am confident we would meet Judas, yes, even Adolf Hitler himself, *had* they humbly engaged in genuine repentance toward the Lord. I hear a gasp. And yet, such is the extent of the mercy of the living God. His love and sympathy are *boundless* toward the contrite heart and soul! Would they experience consequence for their actions? Of course, and rightfully so. But God would receive them with open arms as the father his prodigal son.

God wants to lavish his mercy upon those who love him. He desires to prosper his children. In fact, not only does he do so for our sake, but he blesses us for his *own* sake. When we honor God with our lives, and then thrive from his goodness, protection, and blessing, others take notice. They will begin to perceive the cause and effect relation between fearing God and the prosperity he affords.

When describing the restoration of Israel after their repentance, God says he will place his "fear in their hearts so that they will not depart from Me. Yes, I will rejoice over them to do them good"(Jer. 32:40, 41). God further explains "it shall be to Me a name of joy, a praise, and an honor before all nations of the earth, who shall hear all the good that I do to them; they shall fear and tremble for all the goodness and all the prosperity that I provide for it." (Jer. 33:9). They would serve a radiant testimony of the mercy, might, and goodness of God if only they repented and returned!

God Is Creator

We often wonder why God withholds luxuries or gifts from us, for we see things from a finite and limited viewpoint. God surveys our lives and character from a completely distinct perspective. His purpose is geared toward refining those who love him, whether that entails granting or retaining from his children.

If we imagine the far from perfect analogy of a parent and child relationship, much may be gleaned in the way of understanding God's provision and a sound fear of the Lord. A typical child wants just about everything he sees that might offer enjoyment. But if the parent were to give in to all these demands, great harm would befall that child. A diet consisting of nothing but cakes and cookies and sodas would undoubtedly be detrimental to one's health, so a parent must set consumption boundaries. Even excessive healthy food would lead to a gluttonous lifestyle producing obesity, so limits must be placed. If God merely gave us all we wanted, most of us would quickly spoil and grow distant to the very God whose hand supplies.

God is similar to a parent who provides for his child. But when we introduce the fear of the Lord, how does this relate? Should a child be afraid of his parents? Of course not, not in a healthy family anyway. At the same time, the child should possess a reverence for his parents, as well as a fear of negative consequence that follows disobedient behavior. God extends discipline to his children in order to correct rebellion with the intention of drawing the rebel toward repentance and godly conduct. He does so out of love so the child might escape calamity, or at worst, a rejection of God himself.

God instructs us to honor our father and mother, paralleling the attitude we are to display toward him. We must each realize our place in the world. God is Creator. We are the creature. As we learn to fear the Lord, we begin to trust him more fully. Proverbs boldly promises: "trust in the Lord with all of your heart, and He will make your path straight" (Prov. 3:5, 6). We are God's creation and we must fear him, ironically and interestingly to our own advantage and enjoyment.

Out Of Love

Many reasons stand out as to why we should fear God. God judges between right and wrong, and then dispenses discipline to wrongdoers. We want to avoid divine punishment, so we choose instead to obey God as best we can. But there lies a nobler, more perfect motive for fearing God. As we mature in the knowledge of whom God is and what he has done for us, fear of the Lord will arise from our love for him instead of simply the avoidance of punishment.

It is inevitable. The deeper our love for God grows, the more we shun sin. Obedience should emanate from love for the one whose character we are to shadow. We will love out of a reverence and admiration for God. A desire to please him shall spring forth as our greatest reward as intimacy cultivates between our Creator and us.

As Solomon attests in Proverbs 8, "The fear of the Lord is to hate evil." God detests sin, and as we know and appreciate him more fully, we too will despise and turn aside from immorality.

> He who has My commandments and
> keeps them, it is he who loves Me.
> And he who loves Me will be loved by My Father,
> and I will love him and manifest Myself to him.
> —John 14:21

Jesus submits clear evidence of the man who genuinely loves him. The last thing we want to do is offend God with sin, so from love we submit through obedience. As we develop our love for God, he in turn reveals himself more fully to us.

The fear of the Lord is a lifelong journey as we learn to trust God and increase in faith. We are human and will stumble along the road. But we must rise up, repent of our sins and shortcomings, and continue on.

Jesus claims that he "came that they may have life and have it abundantly" (John 10:10). Jesus came to earth to die for us, that we might know him and discover restoration. His purpose on earth was to extend hope, while rendering us a new, full, and satisfying life. Jesus explains that he is the door of the sheep, the gate for those who trust in him. He describes this door as narrow, with few treading through, though he wished all would walk the path. Blessing comes through *him*, but sadly, few will humble themselves to claim all he offers.

God wants to instill a righteous fear into man so he will neither wander nor fall astray. God does so from the vantage of love, blessing the upright man with the favor of his eyes and ears. "The eyes of the Lord are on the righteous," offering protection and guidance, "and His ears are open to their cry." He knows our every need and hears when we call for help. On the contrary, the "face of the Lord is against those who do evil" (Ps. 34:15, 16). Try as he may, the immoral man will ultimately fail as he contends with God. God wins every time.

We must learn to fear God through obedience. But more than that, as our relationship with God grows in intimacy, we will fear him with joy, springing from our love and thanksgiving for God. Finally, as a further bonus, as if we needed one, we can fear God with expectation, as he promises to reward and pour upon the faithful his shelter, goodness, and favor.

Points To Ponder

- God is perfectly holy and righteous, void of sin, evil intent, or immoral thought.

- God will never compromise his holiness to tolerate rebellion. All sin bears consequences, and a holy God must judge sin.

- God desires that we conform to the character of Christ, set apart and separated from sin.

- When once we begin to understand the holiness of God, it is then we inevitably start to comprehend the fear of the Lord. This reverential fear of his purity will lead to obedience and desire to please him.

- God is actively searching for the faithful few who will turn aside from a life of sin in order to submit and honor him.

- The Lord pities those who fear him. His compassion knows no bounds toward the one who reveres his name and is truly repentant.

- As we mature in the knowledge of who God is and what he has done for us, our fear of the Lord will arise from our love for him.

- God extends discipline to his children in order to correct rebellion with the intention of drawing the rebel toward repentance and godly conduct.

CAN WE TRUST THE ORACLE?

All Scripture is given by inspiration of God,
and is profitable for doctrine, for reproof,
for correction, for instruction in righteousness.
—2 Timothy 3:16

UNFALTERING WORD OF GOD

The promises of prosperity are unmistakably evident throughout Scripture. One may question, however, whether the source may be relied upon. This presents a reasonable question, for if the source of pledge is subject, why should anyone wholly commit to its claims? The truth is, much of the Bible may not be proven, or faith it no longer would be. But be not hasty in your unbelief, for the Word of God has been tried and tested for thousands of years and prevails in consistency and credibility.

It is a matter for each soul to consider whether to trust in its doctrines or upon his own. While the beliefs in the Bible are unproven, per say, they stand regularly confirmed to the individual believer in his encounters to which he attests. With neither personal experience, faith, nor desire for God, the unbeliever cannot fathom the veracity to which the Bible professes. The apostle Paul explains, "But the natural man does not receive the things of the Spirit of God, for they are foolishness to him; nor can he know them, because they are spiritually discerned" (1 Cor. 2:14).

So can we confide in the ancient Scriptures? That is the real issue here. The author of Psalm 119:160 claims, "The entirety of

Your word is truth, and every one of Your righteous judgments endures forever". If the Bible is a sham, then the principles and significance are doubtful, and its value petty. Believers in its philosophies naively waste what scant time they inhabit the earth on deceitful words of hope. On the other hand, if the Bible is trustworthy, it is the unbeliever who dwells in dreadful peril until he perceives his need for God and the deliverance only he can furnish.

If the Word of God is determined valid, the believer *must* also trust the Oracle. They go hand in hand. One may not believe the one and dismiss the other. To remain rational, he trusts in both or else neither. He may not waver between the two if he deem himself at all logical. But be certain, though a person rejects the credibility of God's Word, it by no means deems it invalid. For the Word of God stands on its own, unmoved and unshaken by the whims of man.

Divine Authority Claimed

Many people want the privilege of determining which portions of the Bible they regard as true, and which accounts they may brush aside as fable. Satan loves this vantage, for each person may configure the God of his liking. God transforms into an obscure being somewhere far away, unengaged with the affairs of this world. He is easy and loving, and immeasurably tolerable of the individual's preferred variety of immorality.

Jesus had a different take altogether. He affirmed the truth of the Scriptures by repeatedly quoting passages from the Old Testament. He also confirmed accounts often bearing skepticism, including the chronicles of Jonah and the whale, Noah and the ark, and the judgment upon the cities of Sodom and Gomorrah.

The apostle Paul tells us that "all Scripture is given by inspiration of God" (2 Tim. 3:16). Interestingly, too, are the thousands of instances when the Bible specifically states the expression, "thus says the Lord" or similar diction, to emphasize the conclusive authority of the Word of God.

UNITY OF MESSAGE

Other evidence supporting the validity of the Scriptures and the Oracle stem from an extraordinary unity among approximately forty authors who penned the Bible. Written across a span of 1500 years or so, all sixty-six books and letters that comprise the Word of God share a consistent message and singularity of purpose. Add to this unlikelihood the origins of the authors emerge from diverse cultures, dialects, countries, and distinct walks of life. This miraculous achievement is inconceivable apart from recognizing the direct inspiration of God through his chosen channels of man.

The central message of the Bible is to reveal God's redemptive plan for fallen man. Jesus bore upon himself the sins of the world. He paid the penalty for sin by dying and carrying the full weight of the world's iniquity before rising from the dead. All we must do is trust in his sacrifice on our behalf and follow him.

One noteworthy element of this account is the devotion of the disciples toward their Lord. They and hundreds of others professed to see and converse with Jesus on numerous occasions after he rose from the dead. The disciples faced ruthless pain, torture, and agonizing demises as a result of their claims. Common tradition holds that James was beheaded, Matthew and Thomas were speared to death, Bartholomew, Andrew, Philip, and Simon were crucified, Peter was crucified upside down, Thaddaeus was stoned, James son of Alpheus was tossed from the temple roof, stoned, and his head bashed with a club, and John is believed to have been boiled in oil and exiled to the island of Patmos.

Not many people will die for a *recognized* lie. Few will cling to a sham or hoax to the point of death. In general, people cave in and finally yield to the truth when pressure grows intense, especially when their lives are at stake. The disciples went to the grave clutching to what they had witnessed and experienced firsthand. They stood steadfast and unmoved, for what they believed was real, and they knew it.

Now granted, some people do perish for a lie, no question. But they die trusting in the lie, not realizing that it is, in fact, untrue. Once recognized as inaccurate, these would undoubtedly turn and run the other direction before dying for a counterfeit cause. The disciples faced death confidently, for they had personally seen the Messiah, the Son of God who came for the sole purpose of saving their soul!

Centrality Of Christ

Perhaps not incredibly astounding, it is at least interesting to consider how the central figure of Scripture divides the Bible in two major segments. The Old Testament anticipated and prophesied the coming of Jesus, who would appear to redeem a fallen world. Four hundred years of silence descend like a heavy fog until John the Baptist announces the advent of Jesus, along with his message to repent, turn from our ways, and follow him. The New Testament presents numerous accounts of his life and supreme sacrifice for us, and finally culminates by forecasting the return of Christ one day.

Even more fascinating still, is the arrival of Jesus upon earth bisecting history itself. The entire timetable of human existence from B.C. to A.D. centers upon a loving Creator who became man for our sakes, that we might discover renewed fellowship with God. I find it quite intriguing, that whether regarded or not, much of the secular world inadvertently celebrates both the birth of the Messiah at Christmas and his resurrection from the dead at Easter.

Scores of books are dedicated to establishing the authenticity of the Bible as God's inspired word. We have only touched the surface, and since it is not our primary aim here, I encourage the cynic to investigate and consider the reasoning of those volumes before disregarding the authority of Scripture.

A beautiful attribute of the Word of God is its timelessness. It holds true today and tomorrow, just as certainly as it did thousands of years ago. The Psalms assure us the truths endure to *all* generations. The words of God are immutable and a stronghold, powerful and trustworthy. I hesitate to place any emphasis upon the placement of the central verse in the Bible, so I do not, but I find it interesting nonetheless. Psalm 118:8 boasts the precise midpoint of Scripture and wisely touts, "It is better to trust in the Lord than to put confidence in man."

FULFILLED PROPHECIES

I shall resist the urge to discuss the fulfilled prophecies in any detail, for a comprehensive study would prove exhausting. From the destruction of the cities of Tyre and Jerusalem, the rebuilding of Jerusalem, the captivity of the Jewish people, and the prediction of Elijah's supernatural departure by dozens of prophets, scores of predictions have been confirmed.

Ponder the implications toward a one world currency where credit and smart cards traverse cultural and national boundaries. Consider the ease of the internet, with a simple few clicks, in purchasing virtually anything from around the globe from the convenience of your home. Examine the enhanced efforts toward a one world religion, as tolerance trumps the word of the day and religions pervert truth while endeavoring to unite in the name of peace.

Reflect on the numerous prophecies foretelling the coming of the Messiah, not to mention the precise town of his birth! The betrayal for the price of a slave (thirty pieces of silver) was predicted long before the arrival of Jesus, as well as both the means of his death and resurrection. Contemplate Jesus hanging high upon the cross and crying aloud, "Eli, Eli, lama sabachthani?" which translates, "My God, My God, why have You forsaken Me?" There is no coincidence these words mirror those precisely penned in the Psalm of David, alluding to the Messiah's death hundreds of years prior.

Since Scripture is the inspired Word of God with contents divinely appointed and decreed, and the very nature of God flawless, it goes without saying that the Bible stands inerrant. If reliable, the hundreds upon hundreds of prophecies contained within its pages must hold true. And indeed they have thus far, with hundreds of them bearing fulfillment already, and many more showing signs quickly forthcoming.

SATAN AFFIRMATION

I find it fascinating that our primary adversary in this world unwittingly validates the entire premise of the Oracle. When Satan presented himself before God long ago, the Lord questioned from where he had come. Responding he had been treading back and forth upon the earth, God inquired if he had considered Job. There were no others like Job, God insisted, a righteous man who feared God and turned from evil.

Satan's reply is nothing short of noteworthy. He accuses Job of being upright solely for the sake of benefits received. He led a blameless life toward his own profit. God rendered complete protection around Job and his family and blessed him financially. Job feared God for he knew prosperity would follow in so doing! Satan challenged God to remove the blessings and watch as Job would surely turn in rebellion to the point of cursing him for loss of prosperity.

God allowed Satan a measure of permission to satisfy his test. Calamity struck. Job's servants were murdered and his livestock and finances obliterated. While his ten sons and daughters dined together in the eldest brother's home, a tornado ripped through, collapsing the house and killing them all. Finally, Job's own health was snatched into a life of pain and misery.

Through all this, Job trusted God (Job 1:6—2:10). Satan lost the challenge, and we're told God blessed Job more than he had in the beginning (Job 42:12). Once again, the Lord prospered Job for fearing him regardless of circumstance.

Personal Experience

Without ears, we would discern no sound. Absent eyes, we would have no cognition of color. Lacking a nose, the sensation of smell would remain completely foreign. Devoid taste buds, we would possess no perception of taste.

The suggestion that there exists no spiritual arena is a naive assumption. The spiritual dimension is very much alive and actively engaged amongst the physical realm at any given moment. The fact that we are unable to clearly visualize this dimension merely points to the defined limits mandated upon the physical state we currently reside within. If either were deemed more real than the other, certainly the spiritual domain would triumph, for it existed before us and shall persist long after our inevitable departure.

Possibly the soundest proof in the authenticity of the Bible is discovered in the one who presently exhibits faith. Faith grows as one draws nearer to God in his pursuit and obedience to his precepts. Without submission to God's expressed guidelines, faith dwindles into indifference, or worse, disbelief. Curiously, the one who disbelieves Scripture regards it foolishness to suppose it true, while the one who does believe struggles to comprehend how one could possibly not. "Do you see a man wise in his own eyes? There is more hope for a fool than for him" (Prov. 26:12).

I find it remarkable how God draws the humbled soul to himself, and at the same time, allows a spiritual blindness to confuse the self-sufficient. He never forces a person to trust in him, but gives each individual free will to either pursue or reject him.

Personal experience is first-hand evidence to the believer for the authenticity of the Oracle. You might liken it to a wonderfully breezy afternoon. While the wind blows along unseen, the effects of its presence is unquestioned to the one in its course. The reality of the wind is obvious to the person enjoying its gust. It is similar with the Holy Spirit. Those who internalize the Spirit of God and enjoy an intimate relationship with him recognize the impact of God upon their lives. The effects of the Spirit are all too genuine and life-altering to dismiss as fraud.

Nothing compares to a personal encounter with God. An event may dramatically propel a person's faith, while offering little reform in the life of another. Generally, only the one brushed by God is profoundly impacted and spiritually strengthened. While a person may verbally share an answered prayer or miraculous experience with others, few will reap comparable benefits of the petitioner. Others may be encouraged or mildly inspired, but the external person is rarely touched significantly by the miracles affecting the life of another. He may hear a "that's really neat" or "how amazing," but an experiential gulf exists between the listener and the one with intimate encounter. The bystander generally goes about his normal life grossly unmoved, as the soul in pursuit of God draws nearer still.

POINTS TO PONDER

- With neither personal experience, faith, nor desire for God, the unbeliever cannot fathom the veracity to which the Bible professes.

- The Bible's sixty-six books, penned by around forty authors spanning over 1500 years, share a unified message and singularity of purpose.

- Few people will die for a recognized lie, clinging to a hoax to the point of death.

- The Word of God is timeless, remaining true today and tomorrow, just as certainly as it did thousands of years ago.

- Consequences shadow our behavior, whether good or bad, resulting in blessing or curse.

- A person's faith grows as one draws nearer to God in his pursuit and obedience to his precepts.

- Personal experience is first-hand evidence to the believer for the authenticity of the Oracle.

- Without submission to God's expressed guidelines, faith dwindles into indifference, or worse, disbelief.

- God draws the humbled soul to himself, while simultaneously allowing a spiritual blindness to confuse the self-sufficient.

Paradigm Shift

But seek first the kingdom of God and His righteousness,
and all these things shall be added to you.
—Matthew 6:33

Living For The Moment

I opened the door and my hands trembled in the icy morning air. I squinted into the darkness as I let our Boston Terrier out to use the facilities in the backyard. She hates the cold and generally bolts right back inside the house once she has completed the call of nature. On this particular morning, however, she did not return until I wandered around the yard calling for her. At last, she darted inside, chilly yet pleased, and I noticed she was licking her mouth. I knew immediately what she had done. Bending down and smelling her mouth, my assumption was confirmed. Ally had just enjoyed a quick snack in the yard—her own excrement!

I was shocked. Ally had done this many times before, granted, but not when it was this frigid and cutting. She sacrificed her misery of the wintry elements for the sake of eating her waste. Not only that, I ordered her countless times not to consume the disgusting matter because it makes her sick each time. And so it did. She would eat nothing the following day and would lie in bed all morning and afternoon feeling dismal. It would not be long, though, before she was feeling well enough to repeat her hopeless habit. She would succumb to the delicious temptation every time.

I stood there pondering the situation. How could she again

do that, and so soon after getting well? Surely by now she recognized her affliction as driven from her behavior! Even if it did taste pleasant, as unfathomable as that seems, was becoming ill worth it? Nearly a day of suffering and anguish sacrificed for one meager minute of indulgence? How could she be so foolish? Well, that separates the animal from man, I reasoned. Regardless of degree a dog may assume part of the family, there exposed the gulf.

Suddenly it struck me. It was a small aha moment, but a glimmer of self-revelation nevertheless. I am little different than Ally at times. In fact, we as a people are dreadfully similar to my dog when it comes to gratification or pleasure. We so often live for the instant, unaware or unconcerned of the effects our actions may provoke. We fall in the face of temptation, or worse, we actively seek out the immoral deed. Sexual immorality is pleasurable for a moment, but the Bible likens it to eating dung. The aftermath is putrid, and while physical and emotional effects may sometimes seem averted, blessings are certainly forfeited, and a breach widened between the offender and God.

"As a dog returns to his own vomit, so a fool repeats his folly" (Prov. 26:11). When we continue in sin, the Bible compares us to a dog returning to lap up his puke.

Cause And Effect

I removed a pizza from the oven one evening, set the pizza pan on the stove, and told my seven-year-old daughter, "It's super hot, do *not* touch." Within fifteen seconds, I heard a scream. "What happened?" I quickly turned and asked. "I touched the pan," she winced with furrowed brows. I joke this sums up the Old Testament.

Though she heard me, my daughter failed to heed the warning. The Old Testament is full of warnings ignored by the Israelites, resulting in bitter consequence. God frequently introduces pain or affliction in response to sin as a means of averting poor behavior in the future.

Many are oblivious to any existing relation between our actions and subsequent consequences. These either hold a view that God does not exist, or perhaps he is merely uninvolved in the affairs of man, allowing him to behave as he wills without incurring judgment for his conduct.

Others believe they will get away with the poor behavior unscathed. God will not find out if performed in secret, or he is simply too busy to observe the sins of the world. That would seem rational if only he were not an infinite God. According to the following verse, you have already been caught if you entertain and encourage even sinful thoughts and fantasies. "And there is no creature hidden from his sight but all things are naked and open to the eyes of him to whom we must give account" (Heb. 4:13). Jesus concurred, submitting that "every idle word men may speak, they will give account of it in the day of judgment" (Matt. 12:36).

Because space is not the complete vacuum often perceived, it is conceived that every word ever spoken since the beginning of time as we know it, is still traveling somewhere into space. What a chilling thought! Perhaps even more disturbing is the idea that every deed ever committed is preserved in space as well. As the eye witnesses an image, thanks to the reflection of light, so each action is saved through reflection as it traverses into the beyond. Why must the universe be so damnably vast? But for the sake of the amazing grace of God, I would throw in the towel at once!

God is righteous and desires us to be also. Thus, he has established a cause and effect relationship in the moral world as well as in the physical world. Consequence shadows behavior, whether good or bad, and results in blessing or curse. God tells us that if we obey his commands, he will respond in our favor. But if we disobey and turn away, God will actually work against us, in the hope of drawing us back.

From the formation of this world, God made it clear for his creation to follow him. Upon breathing life into Adam, God commanded him to freely eat of any tree except one. If he ate from the forbidden tree, he was promised death, both physically and spiritually, in severed fellowship with his Maker. A universal spiritual law was introduced upon the sphere. Rebellion would lead to curse. Obedience would lead to prosperity.

"Blessed is the man ... whose delight is in the law of the Lord, and in His law he meditates day and night ... and whatever he does shall prosper" (Ps. 1:1—3). Notice it says *whatever* he does shall prosper. Grand or small, his decisions, actions, and steps will prosper as long as he aligns himself with God and his ways. It also claims whatever he does *shall* prosper. It does not suggest whatever he does *could* prosper, *might* prosper, or even *will probably* prosper. God is able to make bold claims, but often leaves them conditioned upon our intent and behavior.

> Delight yourself also in the Lord,
> and He shall give you the desires of your heart.
> Commit your way to the Lord, trust also in Him,
> and He shall bring it to pass.
> —Psalm 37:4, 5

Remember, God is not out to get us, if you will. He wants to bless us. The entire purpose of God awarding us life was for good. God created us to love him, and that he might love us. How then may we show our love for him? One monumental way is through obedience, like a child toward his mother and father.

Chances are we have supposed a particular behavior worth the risk of correction. We may feel our choice of immoral action merits the looming negative effects. We subconsciously weigh the pros and cons of an action, and decide the consequences are too trivial to necessitate concern. Unfortunately, this conviction is deceptive and illusory. Unfavorable consequences *always* outweigh the benefit or satisfaction. The indulgences are short-lived while the costs linger. Poor choices may repeatedly be reduced to a simple lack of faith. If we employed greater faith, we would recognize the reward for morality surpasses any superficial pleasures received from transgression.

We are never free from the effects of sin in our life. God is righteous and cannot tolerate sin. He must enforce discipline for evil behavior. A holy God *must* impose a penalty for depravity.

I can imagine nothing more dreadful than the chastening from an omnipotent God. Thank God he is merciful! He offers forgiveness and restored fellowship to the soul who is genuinely repentant, to the one who desires and intends to change his ways. Unfortunately, even with forgiveness, there are still consequences for sin. We are naive to believe otherwise.

ENLIGHTENED REASONING

We have nothing to do with our conception, and little to say when death knocks at our door and ushers us through. Yet many believe we are the crux of the universe, it moves on our behalf, and behaves as we determine—that we are, in essence, each a god, our own god, and in full control of our fate.

Focused positive thinking opens the door, they claim, and delivers anything we want: wealth, health, happiness, a better job. Focus intently that you will receive whatever it is you require from the hand of the cosmos. The universe cannot help but grant these desires if only you wish for them hard enough, for the ultimate power stems from within you. Imagine the sheer foolishness of such a notion. A shred of reason ought warn us otherwise. It manifests the wisdom of the world, isolated from God, and it is sheer nonsense!

We are minute, ants in the eyes of God. Imagine an ant believing he maintained control of all circumstances influencing him, or that his fate lie within his power of manipulation. If he wanted to rule above all animals, he need only believe intensely enough and the universe would manifest his wish.

A popular school of thought is presently circulating that

essentially promotes just that. If you desire to be wealthy, merely trust you deserve great wealth and the universe has no option but to draw money toward you. You are a magnet, they affirm, to whatever it is you desire. If you want excellent health, imagine yourself healthy, and you will manifest wonderful health.

A number of wealthy individuals actually trust in this mode of belief, that they manipulated their lofty financial position with positive thinking. How unfortunate those in the majority who also rely on positive thinking, yet boast little money, and are never interviewed for their lack of success.

There is a problem with this manner of thinking. We and the ant are the creature. We do not dictate what the universe does for us. From dust we come, and as dust we leave. The wealthiest person in the world perishes as penniless as the poorest.

A chasm exists between man and God. Our sin has severed close communion with God and we stand in dire need of someone to bridge the gulf. God's Son is that only bridge, who took upon himself the sins of the world, that we might be free from the burden and guilt of sin and enjoy newness of life. We must place our faith in him and walk in the fear of the Lord. "God shows no partiality. But in every nation whoever fears Him and works righteousness is accepted by Him" (Acts 10:34, 35).

God desires that we follow and observe his Oracle. "For as the heavens are high above the earth, so great is His mercy toward those who fear Him; as far as the east is from the west, so far has He removed our transgressions from us. As a father pities his children, so the Lord pities those who fear Him" (Ps. 103:11-13).

Israel's wealthy and wise King Solomon knelt to his knees before the people of Israel and lifted his hands toward heaven. "Lord God of Israel," he prayed, "there is no God in heaven or on earth like you, who keep your covenant and mercy with your servants who walk before you with all their hearts." Can you imagine if we had a leader with that much humility, courage, and integrity? Oh, that we had a leader with such fear of the Lord!

THE COMMON MAN

People want to stand out from the crowd more than ever now. They want to communicate individuality and exemplify anything but commonality in a mundane world. Youth who gravitate toward a goth look are tired of the norm, desiring a darker persuasion. As their outer appearance conceals latent issues within, the goth visage unexpectedly becomes common among their own set of peers. But it stops not with the gothic, for people of all types venture to grasp at their own form of individualism. From increasingly popular tattoos, to finer cars and homes, to the latest clothing styles, people strive to differentiate themselves as distinguished from the next.

The Bible speaks of the common man, and of a God who desires to make him unique. God seeks the person who possesses a heart like his in order to accomplish extraordinary things. He draws them to himself, to be different, to be "a special treasure above all the peoples on the face of the earth" (Deut. 7:6). God calls us to consecrate ourselves toward holiness, literally to be *set apart* from others. "You shall be holy to Me, for I the Lord am holy, and have separated you from the peoples, that you should be Mine" (Lev. 20:26).

To be honest, I find it difficult to fathom why God loves us so much, longing to extend mercy and forgiveness to any who will turn to him. He is by no means a perverse God, endeavoring to manipulate us into becoming robots or slaves for his service. God loves humankind, these exceptional creatures he formed in his image and through whom breathed life. He pursues us that we might become his children. What esteemed honor afforded those with whom God desires to bless!

FEAR GOD, NOT MAN

King Solomon assures the one who trusts in God that he will dwell in safety, but warns that a lure and trap entice those who fear man (Prov. 29:25). Fear the Lord and discover peace and security. God instructed the prophet Isaiah not to fear the threats of man, but to hallow the Lord instead. "Let Him be your fear, and let Him be your dread" (Isa. 8:13). David sheds light in one of his Psalms for the reason the ungodly behave as they do. "An oracle within my heart concerning the transgression of the wicked: There is no fear of God before his eyes" (Ps. 36:1).

God looks at the heart *intent*. If a person is obedient this week simply because he wants a promotion the following week, there is good chance he may not receive it. God is seeking the *life* of obedience, not merely a week for the sake of selfish gain. He is searching for a paradigm shift in the mind and soul of one who pursues him without compromise.

The individual who surrenders a tithe of sort, yet strictly for the selfish purpose of acquiring more than given, lacks the worshipful mindset intended. It calls to mind the claw crane vending machines, where a person inserts a couple of coins for a chance to clutch, with miniature crane arm, a prize worth more than the money vested. The person generally walks away empty-handed and slightly upset, complaining the machine is a rip-off and rigged. "I'm never playing *that* again!" A similar attitude ensues when someone gives and gets not what he wanted in return, and then grumbles that "it wasn't worth it. I'm not doing *that* again!" God examines the heart and seeks a proper spirit.

It is one thing to love God. Much of the world loves God, but more often than not, the love is comparable to the love one feels for a car, a pair of new shoes, or a favorite food. A shallow love is shared, and sadly, a deeper emotion with the shoes or chocolate is maintained, as these have a way of evoking a genuine sense of euphoria. The love for God casually professed, but void of any significant meaning, typifies a manner of love little more than an idea. That person loves in theory only, for it seems the right or trendy notion to adopt. I mean, what believer would readily admit to *not* loving God? He would be ostracized, and a wealth of peer pressure would quickly realign his diction.

It is another thing altogether to be *in* love with God. This person is passionate for God, proactively obeying his commands and truths as faithfully as possible. He runs from sin when it rears its ugly head, and he pursues an uncompromising way of life, even when sacrifice is necessary. What a breath of fresh air to meet a man or woman who possesses an eternal perspective, replete with the fear of the Lord, a zeal for pleasing God, and a fervor for doing what is right no matter what!

It often takes a degree of loss or traumatic event to awaken a person's perception as to what is truly important and worth prioritizing in life. A father wishes he had invested more quality time with his children once they are grown and have moved on. An elderly man on his death bed rarely wishes he had spent more time in the office. Reasoning otherwise would obviously be irrational. His life priorities are now more appropriately aligned. A widow, upon losing a spouse, wishes she had spent more precious moments with her mate. After a catastrophic tsunami struck the shores of Japan years ago, countless survivors were awakened as they discovered what truly is important in life.

THE RADICAL LIFE

Everyone wants to accomplish something spectacular, to be someone outstanding, or to affect the world in some extraordinary manner. We all possess an internal impulse for achieving something great. Incidentally, a prominent hindrance is often ourselves and our world view. What can *I* do to change the world? How can *I* produce a positive outcome? What would stimulate *my* popularity and lend *me* fame?

While not an entirely poor line of questioning, perhaps a more effective mode of discourse would develop from an altered perspective. If we removed us from the source of alteration and surrendered its rightful placement to God, we kindle a more compelling potential for transformation. How can *God* use me to change the world? How can I allow *God* to produce a positive outcome through me? How may I exalt *God* and make *his* name famous? With God at the helm, positive change is exponentially more promising.

Now consider Jesus for a moment and his radical mindset while gracing us with his presence. He behaved differently than the world around him, extending compassion when others refused. Jesus demonstrated surpassing love for man and perfect love for God, humbly sacrificing for the will of his Father. Jesus forgave the grotesque, embraced the offensive, and accepted the unworthy.

Now much of the world misinterprets the purpose of Jesus in eating and associating with sinners at times. He was not accompanying them because he accepted their corrupt lifestyles, as many profess, and thereby demand believers to likewise accept their immorality. Quite the opposite holds true. Jesus despised the sin, yet loved and welcomed the sinner, with every intention of drawing them to repentance and new life. Jesus indeed lived a radical life.

What on earth did Jesus possess that we so desperately require in our lives? *He epitomized an eternal, kingdom perspective!* Our focus is, more often than not, severely misdirected. A radically altered outlook is critical. We must choose to sacrifice our will for the sake of something greater. We must determine to forfeit our immoral desires in the interest of something better. Embracing a life of integrity amidst a perverse world is nothing short of radical.

A paradigm shift in our personal assessment is imperative. We must revolutionize our lives by radically changing perspective if we aspire to see reality more credibly. Hope and prosperity stem not from within ourselves, as much of our culture today claims, but from God. Apart from him, our lives are barren and meaningless. It matters not if we possess superior health and wealth. While an emptiness fills the heart, a void consumes any lasting purpose we may strive to achieve.

Once we internalize this fresh mindset, it will shape and transform us. It is regrettably fascinating how few genuine believers exist in the world. We are called to cling to the one true God and renounce all others, particularly the god of self. Self must be dethroned!

- Poor choices may repeatedly be reduced to a simple lack of faith. If we employed greater faith, we would recognize the reward for morality surpasses any superficial pleasures received from transgression.

- Unfavorable consequences always outweigh any perceived benefit or satisfaction of immoral behavior.

- God is completely and perfectly righteous, and a holy God cannot tolerate sin.

- God offers forgiveness and restored fellowship to the soul who is genuinely repentant, to the one who desires and intends to change his ways.

- Prosperity springs not from within ourselves, as much of our culture claims today, but from God. Apart from the Creator who imparted us life and form, our lives are barren and meaningless.

- God calls us to consecrate ourselves toward holiness, literally to be *set apart* from others. Since he is holy, he requires us to be holy.

- God is searching for a paradigm shift in the mind and soul of one who pursues him without compromise.

- Jesus possessed an eternal, kingdom perspective, that we so critically need. This radically altered perspective is imperative in our life!

A Changed Perspective

The fool has said in his heart,
"There is no God."
—Psalm 14:1

God's Word Is Alive

I used to peruse the Old Testament and ponder the teachings of the ancient Book penned thousands of years ago. I would consider the counsel voiced to the nation of Israel, God's chosen people, and instructions proclaimed to individuals of interest in former times. The stories were interesting, especially assuming part of history, but I grew uninterested and the dust would settle like a blanket of snow upon the antiquated book.

Then something happened one day I shall not soon forget. I entreated God to instill in me a genuine desire to read his Word, rather than from obligation. I recalled one of his countless promises, "If you abide in me, and my words abide in you, ask what you desire, and it shall be done for you" (John 15:7). Another verse concurred, "And whatever things you ask in prayer, believing, you will receive" (Matt. 21:22).

Now I knew my request needed to align with the will of God, and being certain he wanted me to read the Bible, I felt comfortable in my plea. I was shocked when, over the next few days, I began to hunger, truly hunger, for his Word. I actually looked forward to reading the Scriptures! I cannot explain it except for my prayer he so generously answered. His promises are indeed faithful, though they must not contradict his will.

It was another aha moment for me. I never read the Word of God in the same manner again. The Bible was no longer an archaic book written for people who perished generations ago. It was *alive*! God was speaking to *me* just as he had to others centuries before. His promises, I realized, are as pertinent and true today as ever. The letter of Hebrews claims, "For the word of God is living and powerful, and sharper than any two-edged sword, piercing even to the divisions of soul and spirit, and of joints and marrow, and is a discerner of the thoughts and intents of the heart" (Heb. 4:12). Unlike all other books, God's Word is both *living* and *powerful*!

God is the same yesterday, today, and tomorrow, and his precepts have not and shall never change. His promises of blessing for obedience and forewarnings of curses for defiance are as valid now as in the days of Moses. God still wants our submission, calls us to love him wholeheartedly, and requires that we fear him. God longs to prosper us if only we will awaken to him. What he expects from us is not meant to burden us, but rather lighten our bondage in this life. We are not forsaking the joys of life when we follow God. On the contrary, as we abandon our self-absorption to live for him, God works on our behalf. God aspires to profit and benefit us for his glory.

Promises Resurrected

Recognizing the promises of God as valid and reliable today spawned in me numerous additional personal aha moments. The pledges in Scripture I had grown accustomed to hearing were no longer dead. The Creator was speaking to *me*, presently, in the comfort of my living room through his Word. My coldness toward the assurances of God thawed as my excitement intensified. I began to grasp a new potential for my life with a freshly discovered love for God and his purpose for my being.

As a believer's perspective is properly renewed, a paradigm shift to fear the Lord is adopted, paving the way for secondary shifts to pleasantly spring forth.

Honor God And Be Honored By God

> Those who honor Me I will honor,
> and those who despise Me shall be lightly esteemed.
> —1 Samuel 2:30

If I honor the Creator of the universe, he will honor me? How preposterous a concept! I should revere God expecting nothing further in return, for he lent me breath and then yielded his own for mine. And still, he wants to honor *me*, if only I exalt him? What a remarkable promise, nearly too wonderful to believe! Nearly. For I opt to trust him, as his word is ever steadfast. God is the only one perfectly faithful and trustworthy.

A fascinating verse in Genesis reveals God placing his character at stake, as he promises blessing upon an obedient Abraham. "By Myself I have sworn, says the Lord, because you have done this thing, and have not withheld your son, your only son— blessing I will bless you, and multiplying I will multiply your descendants" (Gen. 22:16, 17).

On the contrary, if we rebel against God or contend with his precepts, God will work against us. One may amass adversaries in this world, but God should never be included as one of them. One of the most beautiful and powerful angels supposed otherwise, persuading millions of others to follow in his insurrection. Lucifer did not succeed, and neither shall any who oppose him.

How should we honor God? By holding him in high esteem and high regard. He is worthy of our respect, and deserves precedence above all created persons and things.

I enjoy reflecting upon opposite characteristics of terms in order to grasp a better understanding of the meaning of a particular word. In this instance, to identify more suitably how we are to honor God, one might consider the manner a person might dishonor him. The reader might immediately presume that worshiping an idol would dishonor God. Deifying a carved image would certainly disgrace the Creator, and upon further reasoning, he would realize that setting anything or anyone before God would qualify an idol. To assign more worth to something other than God is to judge it more valuable. Even treasuring a child or spouse above God is unacceptable and offensive, for he remains a jealous God.

But is not jealousy a sin? Indeed, jealousy is immoral when someone is envious of what another person possesses. It does not belong to the jealous individual, and so he covets it for himself. However, when God expresses his jealousy, he is referring to a person assigning another that which *rightfully* belongs to him. God alone merits our worship, and he must occupy top priority in our life if we want for us his best.

How else might a person succeed in dishonoring God? One would rightly assume that disregarding his commandments would promote irreverence. Theft, murder, lying, and adultery are obvious violations and would necessitate a breach in fellowship with the one who is hallowed. Any type of disobedience, rebellion, or unfaithfulness on our part would clearly dishonor a righteous God.

A person could also speculate that avoiding his Maker would prove dishonorable. Fleeing God's will as Jonah fled Ninevah was unmistakably wrong as he soon found himself consumed by a fish. Furthermore, as a husband devoting no time with his wife, so he who neglects God on account of disinterest or indifference would surely be offensive. God finds the lukewarm at heart repulsive. "So then, because you are lukewarm, and neither cold nor hot, I will vomit you out of My mouth" (Rev. 3:16). The picture of his reaction is anything but appealing.

Finally, an individual who refuses to believe in God or his

Word may assume he is disgracing God. The author of Hebrews cautions us, "But without faith it is impossible to please Him, for he who comes to God must believe that He is, and that He is a rewarder of those who diligently seek Him" (Heb. 11:6).

A lack of faith is distasteful to God, for he is eager to open the eyes of any willing to pursue him. Jesus urges us to "ask, and it will be given to you; seek, and you will find; knock, and it will be opened to you. For everyone who asks receives, and he who seeks finds, and to him who knocks it will be opened" (Matt. 7:7, 8).

If anyone desires additional faith, simply ask, seek, and knock. To the insincere, I recommend not bothering to waste his energy and time. But to the persistent and genuine in heart, God will bless with greater and greater measure.

God has never left us to discover him in blind faith though. He has revealed himself to mankind in plentiful ways, including his Word, creation, Son, and even our conscience. "For since the creation of the world His invisible attributes are clearly seen, being understood by the things that are made, even His eternal power and divine nature, so that they are without excuse, because, although they knew God, they did not glorify Him as God, nor were thankful, but became futile in their thoughts, and their foolish hearts were darkened" (Rom. 1:20, 21).

We can choose to continue riding the fence if we wish. We love God, but that is about the extent of the matter, following him when convenient, obeying when beneficial, and avoiding sin as suitable with our desires. But the fence shall remain our home, lukewarmness our friend, and a mundane complacency our norm. Blessing will drift by, ever so close, and yet somehow never attainable. We need only humble ourselves and seek him.

As mentioned, there is a thriving philosophy that exalting *yourself* leads to success and prosperity. Just believe strongly and think enough positive thoughts. You control the power within to alter the universe to move on your behalf. The world revolves around *you*.

Lies, lies, lies! The person who exalts himself will assuredly be humbled, while the meek is ironically uplifted. Listen to what the Lord told Elijah: "See how Ahab has humbled himself before me? Because he has humbled himself before me, I will not bring the calamity in his days" (1 Kings 21:29). The one who humbles himself attracts the attention of God.

GIVE AND YOU SHALL RECEIVE

Jesus inspires us to "give, and it will be given to you: good measure, pressed down, shaken together, and running over will be put into your bosom. For with the same measure that you use, it will be measured back to you" (Luke 6:38). Give little, receive little. Give much, receive much. Few risk the challenge. Using similar reasoning, we might also conclude that much will be withheld from the one who withholds much.

If we really believed this verse, we would give not only joyously, but radically. The same measure used to give will be the same given? Why would anyone hold back if this were the case? We must lack faith, as simple as that.

Obedient actions and behaviors are essential, but often skin-deep. Ultimately, it is the intent of the heart that matters. A vital element is lacking when we provide for the needy, but do so with complaining and resentment. Paul offers encouraging words to inspire us to selfless giving. "But this I say: He who sows sparingly will also reap sparingly, and he who sows bountifully will also reap bountifully. So let each one give as he purposes in his heart, not grudgingly or of compulsion; for God loves a cheerful giver" (2 Cor. 9:6, 7).

We obtain the word "hilarious" from the Greek word for *cheerful*. God loves when a person gives joyfully, even hilariously, with a passion for helping another. If we cringe while donating our hard-earned money toward the purposes of God, we have yet to arrive at the hilarious giving of which God speaks. And not to be too harsh, for the act of giving does display obedience, and in that God is pleased, even with the one who might do so hesitantly. It is a starting point, for certain, but that individual has further to travel. "You shall surely give to him, and your heart should not be grieved when you give to him, because for this thing the Lord your God will bless you in all your works and in all to which you put your hand" (Deut. 15:10).

The Proverbs are rich in promises concerning generosity and assisting the poor. Consider the following verse to inspire cheerful charity. "He who has a generous eye will be blessed, for he gives of his bread to the poor" (Prov. 22:9). Other promises are more daunting, including an undesirable pledge to the noncompliant. "He who gives to the poor will not lack, but he who hides his eyes will have many curses" (Prov. 28:27).

How will a person know when he is giving enough? That is a question for each individual to determine, for the answer will vary from one to another. If one withholds from sharing, yet his conscience expresses otherwise, he may need to reevaluate his position. I stand convinced in one piece of advice, though. For the one claiming no money to give, it is he specifically who cannot afford *not* to give! Begin small if you must, but reach within and give sacrificially through faith.

Giving should be a sacrifice. If rendering something is not felt, perhaps more should be surrendered. Sacrifice one meal out of twenty-one per week if nothing else, but step out in obedience and give *something*. Just remember, the less we entrust to God, the less we are entrusted. "There is one who scatters, yet increases more; And there is one who withholds more than is right, but it leads to poverty. The generous soul will be made rich, and he who waters will also be watered himself" (Prov. 11:24, 25).

The almighty dollar boasts a powerful grip on man. Whether a person has little or abundance, the influence of money is strong and requires discipline to relinquish. But make no mistake, for giving is not an option with God. It is a command, as God instructs us to sacrifice by way of tithes and offerings.

Listen to the personal affront toward God as he warns man of his selfishness, and yet offers grace and prosperity to the one who will choose obedience through sacrifice. When God plainly accused the Israelites of robbing him, they were shocked. "In what way have we robbed You?" they asked. "In tithes and offerings," God replied. "You are cursed with a curse, for you have robbed Me ... bring all the tithes ... and try Me now in this," challenged the Lord, "if I will not open for you the windows of heaven and pour out for you such blessing that there will not be room enough to receive it" (Mal. 3:8-10).

To surrender something of value is a shrewd investment. Not only is it liberating physically, mentally, and spiritually, but it brings with it much reward. "But do not forget to do good and to share, for with such sacrifices God is well pleased" (Heb. 13:16). God has commanded us to give, and deciding otherwise brings a curse. How awesome a God who will turn that curse into blessing if only we choose to honor him first!

One last side note on giving before moving on. God wants us to give without others knowing about it. "But when you do a charitable deed, do not let your left hand know what your right hand is doing, that your charitable deed may be in secret; and your Father who sees in secret will Himself reward you openly" (Matt. 6:3, 4). I find this verse riveting. When we give and others take notice, their attention is our reward. There is a much better way. When giving in secret, an inner joy that would otherwise remain dormant, is suddenly stirred and animated. And in reality, since he sees everything, *God* is now the rewarder, and he delights in blessing *publicly*.

Forgive And Be Forgiven

Dwelling in a depraved state, man has continually gorged himself upon illicit pleasures and impure indulgences. We are each at fault, as Romans 3:23 affirms, "all have sinned and fall short of the glory of God." Perhaps someone could assert otherwise if only 1 John 1:8 had not stressed so plainly, "if we say that we have no sin, we deceive ourselves, and the truth is not in us." We are all guilty of despicable sins in the eyes of God.

It gets worse. Romans 6:23 warns, "the wages of sin is death," suggesting a spiritual death and separation from God. God demands a perfect and unblemished sacrifice to pay the penalty for sin. And thus, Jesus was put to death one fateful afternoon that we might acquire eternal life, if only we believe (John 3:16). As Jesus assumed the guilt for the sin of the world, God withdrew, and the skies mourned in darkness that afternoon.

And yet, Jesus forgave his murderers while fighting for breath upon the cross. He waited not for their remorse. He is ready today to forgive any who come with repentant and humble heart. He cleanses and restores the ready soul with fresh perspective and newness of purpose. But the sinner must be willing. He must be repentant. He must be genuine.

It is easy to say we forgive someone, and we may delude ourselves into believing that we actually have done so. But we must ask ourselves if there remains bitterness toward the offender. If so, it is highly probable we have yet to fully forgive. Do we wish vengeance upon the wrongdoer? If so, it is almost certain we have not forgiven. When you forgive, you let go. Anger disappears, bitterness dissolves, and resentment fades. Peace prevails and renews. Releasing these burdens fosters improved health and frees the mind of unwelcome stress and tension.

It may take time, necessitating meditation upon our feelings and the situation, but we need to attain a place of sincere forgiveness. Will we forget the insult or transgression? Hopefully time will heal even the memory of wrongdoing, but oftentimes not, for sin has a way of leaving a scar of remembrance, as it did upon the hands of Christ even after rising from the dead.

Mark 11:25 cautions, "if you hold anything against anyone, forgive him, so that your Father in heaven may forgive you your sins". When we approach God with sincere repentance, God is faithful to forgive. When we forgive others, God will likewise forgive us. "But if you do not forgive men their trespasses, neither will your Father forgive your trespasses" (Matt. 6:15). What a frightening truth that should provoke us to liberate the injustices of man brought upon us. God wants to forgive and free us from sin. But we must pardon others and confess our own rebellion.

Forgiving when others have wronged us can prove challenging. And yet, God compels us further. We are not instructed to like, but to *love* our enemies and do good to them. Talk about a radical shift required in our reasoning! But it will be worth it all, for "then your reward will be great" (Luke 6:35).

Judge Not And Be Not Judged

There is something intrinsically satisfying about judging another. A self-gratifying quality emerges in pronouncing judgment upon someone else that compels us to feel better about ourselves. Even if the judgment is merely an opinion we quietly hoard within our mind, it is nevertheless an assessment of that person's character and value, or lack thereof. As we brood over the blemishes in others, our estimation of them dwindles, and simultaneously, our own ascends. The resilient weed of pride takes root in the heart, and it shall prove a battle to uproot. Like a drug, the charm of criticism grows routine until we are unaware of its residence upon our character.

Jesus expounds on the corollary between the one condemning and the judgment he shall receive. "Judge not, that you be not judged. For with what judgment you judge, you will be judged; and with the measure you use, it will be measured back to you. And why do you look at the speck in your brother's eye, but do not consider the plank in your own eye? Or how can you say to your brother, 'Let me remove the speck from your eye'; and look, a plank is in your own eye? Hypocrite! First remove the plank from your own eye, and then you will see clearly to remove the speck from your brother's eye" (Matt. 7:1—5).

We would be wise to recognize our personal shortcomings, that we might offer mercy more swiftly to others. Severe warnings caution the hypocritical and those blind of their own offenses. "And do you think this, O man, you who judge those practicing such things, and doing the same, that you will escape the judgment of God?" (Rom. 2:3).

The rhetorical question implies an obvious and resounding, "No!" One cannot shield himself from God's judgment if he hurls similar blame upon another. "There is one Lawgiver, who is able to save and to destroy. Who are you to judge another?" (Jas. 4:12). There is only one who may pronounce condemnation, one Judge alone.

God dispensed hunger upon Israel for their defiance. They ignored him. He sent drought, but again they neglected him. Mildew and a plague of devouring locusts arrived, but to no avail. God sent a plague in the likeness of Egypt, killing young men and horses by sword, so many that the stench of their camps wafted into their nostrils. Again they rejected God's correction. Five times God counters their headstrong hearts with, "Yet you have not returned to Me." Rebellion and sin are an affront to God. He is merciful and forgiving, but he is also Judge. He closes with a stern warning of judgment, "Prepare to meet your God, O Israel!" (Amos 4:6—12).

HUMBLE YOURSELF AND BE EXALTED

God enjoys accomplishing his will against the norm in order to display his splendor. He reveals that if you want to be first, you must be last. God detests pride, the principal reason for the fall of Lucifer and the millions of angels who from heaven trailed. Proverbs 16:18 could not have expressed the adage more plainly, "Pride goes before destruction, and a haughty spirit before a fall."

Conversely, God loves to honor the lowly in spirit. Jesus said, "For whoever exalts himself will be humbled, and he who humbles himself will be exalted" (Luke 14:11). God himself became a modest man, born in a dirty manger, in order to be spit upon, beaten, and nailed to a cross to die for his fallen creation. God is affectionate for the humble in heart and his attention is aroused toward the meek. "But on this one will I look: on him who is poor and of a contrite spirit, and who trembles at My word" (Isa. 66:2).

God enjoys demonstrating his strength and glory when we are weak and desperate. He desires to remove our self-sufficiency that we might rely upon him *alone*. Who better to be in control? We are here today and gone tomorrow, while God retains our soul and eternity in his hands. The infinite Being, who cannot be confined within this world or the heavens, reveals to us the nature of his present abode. "For thus says the High and Lofty One who inhabits eternity, whose name is Holy: I dwell in the high and holy place, with him who has a contrite and humble spirit" (Isa. 57:15).

God longs for us to humble ourselves as young children and pursue him with diligence. He yearns to mend our relationship with himself as he originally intended. He insists, "If My people ... will humble themselves, and pray and seek My face, and turn from their wicked ways, then I will hear from heaven, and will forgive their sin and heal their land" (2 Chron. 7:14). When once we decide to follow him, individually or nationally, God stands ready to forgive the meek with unrivaled compassion.

God wants to exalt his people, all those who have purged their conceit. Lest one mistake this to suggest we endure an insecure, dejected, or depressed existence, I affirm the contrary. For in God we boast strength, freedom, and newness of life! But in him *alone* do we boast.

> Humble yourselves under the mighty hand of God,
> that He may exalt you in due time.
> —1 Peter 5:6

SHOW MERCY AND RECEIVE MERCY

We have all wished for mercy at one point or another. How refreshing when someone generously showers us with kindness in a time of need. Like a glass of cool water satisfying a parched thirst, sympathy is a welcomed friend during a period of adversity. How deplorable, though, when we are quick to seek mercy from God, while slow in extending compassion toward others.

Recognized today as the "Golden Rule", Jesus charged us with a simple, yet compelling command. "Whatever you want men to do to you, do also to them, for this is the Law and the Prophets" (Matt. 7:12). The moral principles from the Old Testament are bundled up and effortlessly summed up in this one philosophy. Similar attitudes existed prior to this, but with a negative slant. "Do *not* harm or do unto others as you would *not* want to be done unto you," was the prevalent stance. Jesus broadened this idea by placing a positive and proactive spin on it. He directs us to do well unto others, not merely the absence of bad.

The Bible speaks much on the subject of showing empathy toward those in need. King Solomon cautions regarding our treatment of the poor. "He who oppresses the poor reproaches his Maker, but he who honors Him has mercy on the needy" (Prov. 14:31). He who offers compassion exalts the Lord, and we know that God honors those who hold him in high esteem. On the contrary, the one who burdens the deprived individual is a disgrace to God.

Another proverb concurs and puts it this way, "He who gives to the poor will not lack, but he who hides his eyes will have many curses" (Prov. 28:27). God observes our behavior concerning his creation and takes offense at our harshness or indifference toward it. Again, the common theme of blessing and cursing arises according to our obedience or lack thereof for the needy.

If we stand faithful to God in our dealings with the underprivileged, he promises to bless us richly in return. "If you extend your soul to the hungry and satisfy the afflicted soul, then your light shall dawn in the darkness, and your darkness shall be as the noonday. The Lord will guide you continually, and satisfy your soul in drought, and strengthen your bones" (Isa. 58:10, 11). God promises to direct our steps, provide our lives with clarity of purpose, and extend good health to our bodies.

God also assures protection and help to the merciful soul. "Blessed is he who considers the poor; the Lord will deliver him in time of trouble" (Ps. 41:1). It is commonly said that if we are not presently experiencing a trial, we either just passed through one or adversity is about to occur. Conflicts are inevitable. It is no small affair to have God on your side when struggles surface.

Yet another proverb encourages us in the virtue of philanthropy. "He who has pity on the poor lends to the Lord, and He will pay back what he has given" (Prov. 19:17). It calls to mind the verse in Hebrews where we are instructed to "entertain strangers, for by so doing some have unwittingly entertained angels" (Prov. 13:2). James challenges us to live a life distinct and set apart from the world. He describes an unpolluted faith toward God in this way: "to visit orphans and widows in their trouble, and to keep oneself unspotted from the world" (Jas. 1:27). He calls us to be distinguished from the world as a light in darkness.

Our life is a testimony to others as we seek to mirror the character of Christ. We should live morally and love our brothers beyond what the norm of mankind is accustomed. What better way than to care for the poor, the orphan, and the widow? The orphan and widow were in severe peril if they had no one to help them, and they typically had no way of repaying anyone. It is easy to help a person when you know you will receive something in return. But we are called to stand out from the rest of the world, to be light and salt of the earth. We are called to be radical, and move beyond what the world is inclined to do.

Isaiah tells us that God shows mercy on those who are merciful, and he acts shrewdly toward those who are conniving. God will rescue the humble, and yet, the arrogant will be brought low. God sees and knows all things. What a wonderfully, fearful persuasion!

- As the paradigm shift to fear the Lord is faithfully adopted, secondary shifts inevitably spring forth from the individual's fresh perspective.

- The Word of God is alive and as pertinent today as ever. His precepts have not and shall never change.

- Hold God in high esteem and in high regard, and he will honor you.

- God observes the heart of man to bless the one who willingly gives sacrificially and joyfully.

- God wants to both forgive and free us from sin. But *we* must pardon others and confess our own rebellion.

- The measure we use to judge others will likewise be used against us.

- God is compassionate and affectionate for the humble in spirit, and toward the one who trembles at his word.

- God stands ready to forgive and shower the meek with unrivaled compassion and blessing.

- God shows mercy to the merciful, and acts shrewdly toward the conniving. God rescues the humble, and brings low the arrogant.

THE ORACLE FOR LIFE

Happy is the man who finds wisdom …
length of days is in her right hand,
in her left hand riches and honor.
—Proverbs 3:13, 16

NEWNESS OF LIFE

God is the giver of life. Every living thing owes its existence to the grand Creator, for devoid of God we are but nothing and all life would promptly cease.

When God created this world, he formed man in his image. What an extraordinary honor bestowed upon humankind, a privilege unrealized by any other creature. Man reveled in the bountiful provisions of his Maker in the Garden of Eden. He lacked nothing and enjoyed close fellowship with God. Genesis describes the Lord as walking about the garden in the cool of the day. God was well-pleased in his creation. Man dwelt in prosperity.

Needless to say, such bliss was short-lived. The moment sin polluted mankind, things changed drastically. A dark curse painted the world and all life on earth suffered its stain. The loveliest rose sprouted thorns, the cunning snake grew legs no more, and man suddenly bore shame in his nakedness. All of creation grieved the effects of the Fall.

This was never the intention of God, who awarded man a soul to enable an intimate relationship with himself. Yet, we have all sinned and bear the curse of severed fellowship. Thankfully, Jesus endured the sins of man upon himself, that man might live anew. There exists no greater love than that. Without Christ, there is no hope for man.

The offer God extends is spectacular. While simple to gain the favor of God, it remains problematic for the majority of people to attain it. If a person trusts that Jesus paid the penalty for his sin and pursues the fear of the Lord, he shall enjoy the favor of God. But his heart must be *genuine*.

There lies the crux of the matter and the quandary for so many individuals. For as simple and uncomplicated as it may be to receive the blessings of God, it is problematic for the one who seeks the rewards and goodness of God alone. The insincere impostor may not gain the approval of God, for God comprehends his intention, and no volume of external deeds can access the favor of God without internal transformation of his soul. He possesses not the spiritual capacity to intimately know God, for he has yet to become a child of God.

Prosperity In Fearing God

The moment a person places his trust in Jesus as Lord and Savior, something miraculous happens. He is spiritually born anew. The gulf formerly conceived by sin between man and God is at last bridged by faith. He is now capable of pleasing God. The Bible makes clear that, "without faith it is impossible to please Him, for he who comes to God must believe that He is, and that He is a rewarder of those who diligently seek Him" (Heb. 11:6).

That is the beginning, the foundation, of a new life and fresh start. It takes neither good works nor church attendance to secure salvation. Never fall for the false hope in attending church, for in no way does the church make you a Christian, as the American visiting China fails to make him Chinese. A repentant heart leading to faith in the Son is all that is required. And if that were all that we ever received from God, it would prove magnificently more than we ever deserve. But he offers so much more to the soul who hungers for him. God guarantees eternal life that begins today, and to those inclined, he proposes an abundant life *now*!

King Solomon instructs the reader of Proverbs to keep its commands, for peace and long life will follow those who comply (Prov. 3:1, 2). A humbling of ourselves is essential in order to sacrifice our personal desires and submit to the morals and parameters set forth.

> You shall walk in all the ways which
> the Lord your God has commanded you,
> that you may live and that it may be well with you,
> and that you may prolong your days in the land
> which you shall possess.
> —Deuteronomy 5:33

Unanswered Prayer

God wants to provide and care for his children; after all, he is the Good Shepherd. A shepherd's role includes affording protection and whatever else his sheep may need. If a sheep ventures off, he diligently pursues in order to draw it back into the fold. God does the same, setting roadblocks and dispensing discipline that we might return. The shepherd carried both a rod and staff while tending the sheep, the rod for protection, and a staff for guidance. The analogy is beautifully portrayed in the Psalms: "The Lord is my shepherd; I shall not lack ... Your rod and Your staff, they comfort me" (Ps. 23:1, 4).

The Bible speaks of the Lord as a guide as well as a rear guard for his children. He is a light for their path and a shield from harm. But be cautioned, for it is clear that God hears only the bleating and prayers of his flock, along with the genuine prayers of a repentant spirit. John assures us, "God does not hear sinners; but if anyone is a worshiper of God and does His will, He hears him" (John 9:31). He hears the person who loves him. Now since we are all sinners, a change must take place in order for us to be viewed as righteous. Jesus is the door that ushers in this holiness on our behalf, which apart from him remains shut.

People regularly feel as if God does not answer their prayers, citing they seem unable to reach beyond the ceiling. Certainly there exists a wealth of reasons for unanswered prayer. Sometimes they are answered, but not in the manner we wanted. Other times, our selfish aim is the hindering factor. But I believe the bulk of prayers go unanswered for the simple reason that they are *not* heard.

What! Does God not hear all prayers? It would sound pleasant to say that indeed he does. But do not forget, sin isolates man from God. The Bible warns, "your iniquities have separated you from your God; and your sins have hidden His face from you, so that He will not hear" (Isa. 59:2). God must distance himself from that which is unholy. If we live in habitual sin, we forfeit close fellowship with the Lord.

The Bible says, "The Lord is far from the wicked, but He hears the prayer of the righteous" (Proverbs 15:29). The "but" makes it easy for the rational reader to deduce that God does not hear the prayer of the wicked. So the prayers of the outwardly immoral man go unheard. What about the individual who constantly performs good works? We need to remember God sees differently than man, for God looks inwardly. The Bible alleges, "If I regard iniquity in my heart, the Lord will not hear" (Ps. 66:18).

We can do all the right things externally, yet if the intent of our heart is corrupt, communion with God is severed. Most of the world misses this point, as the reproof rarely escapes the confines of the pulpit. If we wish to restore intimacy with God, we must confess our sins with *a will to turn* from them.

DIVINE PROTECTION

God intends to protect his people, but conveys a caution to those who spurn him. Be it a sole person or an entire nation casting him off, the consequences are similar. Each forfeits divine protection and is vulnerable to all kinds of trials. When the Israelites contemplated attacking their enemies, the Amalekites, Moses opposed the idea. "Do not go up, lest you be defeated by your enemies, for the Lord is not among you," warned Moses. "Because you have turned away from the Lord, the Lord will not be with you" (Num. 14:42, 43). They were not following God at the time, and Moses knew they would be fighting alone without the security of the Lord.

So what did they do? They refused to listen, and instead, attacked the Amalekites and were defeated. The same happens today. Devoid of God, we struggle to achieve things our way, and so we fail. Why did God allow that to happen, we ask ourselves?

On another occasion, God told the Israelites he would hide his face if they set up idols. "My anger shall be aroused against them," he warned, "and many evils and troubles shall befall them, so that they will say in that day, 'Have not these evils come upon us because our God is not among us?'" (Deut. 31:17). God was unmistakably clear shortly after: "I will heap disasters upon them; I will spend My arrows on them" (Deut. 32:23). Remember, God was addressing his chosen people whom he loved. A stubborn and unruly heart must be refined and purified. There must be sincere repentance in the spirit of man or in the heart of a nation in order to rediscover the presence and goodness of God.

Disobedience breeds strife, friction, and dysfunction. Conversely, obedience spawns peace, harmony, and triumph. The Bible instructs to "do what is right and good in the sight of the Lord, that it may be well with you" (Deut. 6:18). God sees all things, including actions performed in secret, as well as thoughts meandering in the dark recesses of the mind. We can live victoriously as we choose godliness over immorality, and in so doing, we surprisingly command an extraordinary influence in the outcome of our lives. What an inspiration to conduct ourselves with decency and integrity as God intends.

God shielded Daniel when he was cast into the lion's den.

Though hungry, the lions did no harm to the man who exalted his Lord. When King Darius removed Daniel from the den, he finally recognized God as Lord over all. Daniel's accusers were then tossed into the den and immediately devoured by the lions before any struck the floor. God holds authority over all creation and the power to shape the framework of our lives. King Darius acknowledged the principle of the Oracle and boldly ordered the following decree throughout the land:

> I make a decree that in every dominion of my kingdom
> men must tremble and fear before the God of Daniel.
> For He is the living God, and steadfast forever;
> His kingdom is the one which shall not be destroyed,
> and His dominion shall endure to the end.
> —Daniel 6:26

The king was so confident life revolved around the fear of the Lord, he required everyone to submit to the one true God.

TRUST GOD AND GAIN SECURITY

A young child finds herself separated from her mother in a crowded mall, with strangers milling all around. Panic strikes! The terror of knowing no one and being lost from her mom is petrifying. Her heart pulsates faster and faster, eyes darting this way and that. Each stranger threatens, looming high above the girl, her world replete with danger. She begins to cry. She is deserted, scared, and alone.

Suddenly, the mob parts and the child spots her mommy in the near distance. Nothing else matters presently as her fears melt away. The girl races toward the one she loves most dearly, leaping into the open arms of her mother who stoops down to catch her. With complete trust, the girl clings and hugs with all her might. She is safe! All is well.

For the one who trusts in God, the feeling is much the same. God gives a peace difficult to fathom for the person who has yet to taste of it. Once again, it all hinges upon the fear of God. The child and parent analogy is obvious in the following scripture. "In the fear of the Lord there is strong confidence, and His children will have a place of refuge. The fear of the Lord is a fountain of life, to turn one away from the snares of death" (Prov. 14:26, 27).

God grants protection as well, permitting no harm except which he allows first to pass through his palms. "The fear of the Lord leads to life, and he who has it will abide in satisfaction; he will not be visited with evil" (Prov. 19:23).

God never promises a problem-free life, but always the ability to endure what he places along one's path. "Because he has set his love upon Me, therefore I will deliver him … I will be with him in trouble … with long life I will satisfy him" (Ps. 91:14—16). He will never abandon the faithful soul, even amidst the threatening storms one may weather. What a joy to rest in the sovereign arms of God as we weather the ups and downs in this volatile world.

Not only will God remain our guardian during perilous times, he will take the *offense* on behalf of the one who loves him. Joshua ensured the Israelites, "One man of you shall chase a thousand, for the Lord your God is He who fights for you, as He promised you. Therefore, take careful heed to yourselves, that you love the Lord your God" (Josh. 23:10). One man shall chase a thousand! God fights *for* the man in whom he favors.

In fact, not only does he fight for his favored child who has drawn near, God actually becomes an enemy to his enemies, and an opponent to his adversaries (Exod. 23:22). That is like having the biggest and strongest bodyguard following you wherever you go. But even that is a poor analogy. A slightly better comparison, though still unjustly represented, would be to possess a thousand bodyguards surrounding all sides. David avows the "angel of the Lord encamps all around those who fear Him, and delivers them" (Ps. 34:7).

There is neither threat nor trial too great for God to lead us through. At the same token, no affliction or challenge is too minuscule or mundane for God to intervene. God will fight for his people, whether in battle, the workplace, traffic, or the grocery store. Many believe God is too busy or uninterested in the smaller details of life. Nonsense! He is God almighty! Why would we ever place our trust in anyone or anything else?

The Lord fights for those who honor him, and he works against those who dishonor him. While God offers security to the man who fears the Lord, he withdraws his protection from the one who fears him not. Even more daunting, God instigates adversity into the lives of those who reject him. The Bible says, "the people spoke against God ... so the Lord sent fiery serpents among the people" (Num. 21:5, 6). There exists a cause and effect relationship either way, whether an individual pursues or turns from God.

> The fear of the Lord leads to life,
> and he who has it will abide in satisfaction;
> he will not be visited with evil.
> —Proverbs 19:23

Fear God and it will be well with you, we are repeatedly promised throughout the Word of God. If we listen to God, we will live in safety and security, void of the fear of evil. Those who fear not the Lord will "eat the fruit of their own way, and be filled to the full with their own fancies" (Prov. 1:31, 33). Protection is removed as they are left to their own devices.

ACQUIRE A HEART

Not only does the man who fears the Lord do so from obedience, he does so out of love. Psalm 112:1 says the man who delights in the commandments of God will be blessed. He honors God, not from duty, but from the joy he receives in pleasing God. He eagerly follows the ways of God.

God appealed to Moses regarding the Israelites, "Oh, that they had such a heart in them that they would fear Me and always keep all My commandments, that it might be well with them and with their children forever!" (Deut. 5:30). The Israelites experienced a perpetual cycle in regards to the blessing of God. After compromising their morals, they would plummet into despair. Difficult times and ruin plagued them again and again as they drifted from God. Finally, when they could bear it no more, they would repent and return to God. Mercifully, God would forgive and provide a sense of restoration and healing.

God sometimes credits the Israelites for possessing a *mind* for God, yet not acquiring a *heart* for him. They wanted to follow God in theory, but not to the point of sacrificing their selfish passions toward a wholehearted commitment.

Believers, more often than not, behave the same way today. We love God, and yet, something lures us away, be it money, peer pressure, work, selfish desire, or control. We compromise integrity and spiral further and further from a proper relationship with God. Our intimacy, protection, and favor with God is slowly forfeited until the unexpected happens. We lose our job. A loved one dies. Sickness, financial peril, divorce, depression, or other tragedy befalls, and we suddenly find ourselves desperate with nowhere to turn. We look to God. He is always ready to forgive and welcome us back. We rediscover hope, and with God we arise from the mire. Circumstances improve and we again grow self-sufficient as our perceived need for God dwindles, until challenging times assume their role once more.

God advises the unbeliever to heed his wisdom and "turn at my rebuke" (Prov. 1:23). When they choose otherwise and repeatedly reject God, it is a dreadful matter. Once God stretches his hand upon the sinner, and he receives neither regard nor repentance, he will turn away.

Terror, destruction, distress, and anguish will descend upon the sinner. The personified wisdom of God warns, "they will call upon me, but I will not answer; they will seek me diligently, but they will not find me. Because they hated knowledge and did not choose the fear of the Lord ... they shall eat the fruit of their own way" (Prov. 1:28, 29, 31). There is a much better way to live! We all desire safety and security. Unfortunately, few will listen, and divine protection is removed from those unyielding.

Trust God And Gain Guidance

The one who trusts in riches, will in the end, be sorely disappointed. Wealth in this life is short-lived, squandered or lost, and ultimately unsatisfying. The individual who places all hope in a person will also be disheartened at some point, probably sooner than later. The best of mankind struggles with hypocrisy and self-centeredness, and will eventually let down the one who confides in them. Moreover, those who place their confidence in themselves will wind up internally bankrupt when they finally recognize the sham their self-assurance has always been. Their secret is a lie, and their alleged autonomy and supreme influence upon the world to act on their behalf will be exposed as a pitiful charade.

The Oracle, in contrast, beckons the observer to trust fully in God *alone*. It promises guidance to the one who depends upon the Lord. The Proverbs instruct, "Trust in the Lord with all your heart, and lean not on your own understanding; in all your ways acknowledge Him, and He shall direct your paths" (Prov. 3:5, 6). God vows to lead us if we place our faith in him. It signifies a conditional promise, requiring our obedience prior to God's blessing of direction. Difficult situations will surface in our lives we will not completely understand. These challenging times are when we need most to lean upon the perfect comprehension and omniscience of God.

If we do not believe God can manage our predicaments, how can we deem *ourselves* worthy of handling them? "Who among you fears the Lord? Let him trust in the name of the Lord and rely upon his God" (Isa. 50:10).

Points To Ponder

- No volume of external deeds can access the favor of God without the internal transformation of his soul.

- The individual who has yet to become a child of God does not possess the capacity to know God intimately.

- The gulf conceived by sin between man and God is bridged only by faith in the death and resurrection of Christ.

- If we wish to restore intimacy with God, we must confess our sins with intent to turn from them.

- Divine protection is forfeited when a person rejects God and his ways.

- There must be sincere repentance in the spirit of man, or in the heart of a nation, to rediscover the presence and goodness of God.

- A holy God will not prosper that which is unholy.

- While God offers security to the man who fears the Lord, he withdraws his protection from the one lacking reverence.

- Those who place their confidence in themselves will wind up internally bankrupt when they finally recognize the sham their self-assurance has always been.

THE ORACLE FOR PURPOSE

Delight yourself also in the Lord,
and He shall give you the desires of your heart.
Commit your way to the Lord, trust also in Him,
and He shall bring it to pass.
—Psalm 37:4, 5

DESIRES OF YOUR HEART

We all have deep-seeded passions we sense our soul tugging us to pursue. It may be a purpose we feel inclined to fulfill or achieve. Many of these desires remain good, moral, and healthy. These we may strive to attain, providing they fit within God's plan for our lives. Other aspirations are not as wholesome or beneficial, often-times ill wrought, suggesting darker lusts in need of suppression.

Far be it for a longing to be a sinful idea, though, so long as it reflects a worthy desire. God himself is a God of considerable passion. To hunger for God is not simply noble, but a quality he actively seeks from his people. Spending time in communion with the Lord through prayer and exploring his Word are logically admirable cravings.

But what about those yearnings which obscure the lines between the obviously spiritual and good, and the physical wants only beneficial in this present physical sphere of life. Are these deemed good or bad? Certainly it will depend on the priorities of an individual and the intentions of the longings pursued. Do the desires move a person nearer to God, or rather hinder his relationship in some way? Has God precedence in the person's life, or do his behaviors follow the dictates of his own aspirations?

As a soul seeks God, desires will gradually transform to those which God adores. The more intimately the person knows God, the further his wants will shift. The appeal to follow after sin will diminish as his Lord becomes top priority. He recognizes the primary purpose in life is to live for his Creator, to bring glory to his name, and to grow in his likeness and character.

But still his heart longs for things in this world, be it possessions, a spouse, children, a vacation, or even rest. God promises to provide for all of our needs, and he is gracious to afford those things which are pleasing and coincide with his will for our lives. The opening verse in this chapter boldly claims that God will grant your desires, but only if conditions are met. It is a conditional promise, so we must first do our part. Again, God will not be regarded as a genie in a bottle, to be dusted off whenever we demand something of him. He is no servant. Nor may he be reduced to a theorem, whereby, when we have met all criteria, he must respond to our wishes. He is no fool. He knows what is beneficial for us and what will prove destructive. Thankfully, he withholds many of our egocentric wants.

So what are the conditions we must uphold? They are presented plainly. We are to delight ourselves in the Lord, discovering real joy and pleasure in knowing him. When once we recognize all God has done and continues doing for us, our commitment and obedience heighten. We begin to enjoy his ways, and with this newfound allegiance we learn to trust God more fully. Our love for the Lord grows and faithfulness naturally follows.

Another point worth mentioning is the word *shall* from the verse above. Twice it is used, once assuring the reader God will grant his desires as he delights in the Lord, and the other ensuring God will bring the faithful one's ways to pass. Consider what it does not say. It does not say God *might* give the desires of your heart, nor *possibly*, nor even *probably*. The claim is bold and confident. He *shall* grant the devoted soul the desires of his heart!

SUCCESS IS CONDITIONAL

The introduction to the Book of Psalms establishes this standard in the initial three verses. "Blessed is the man whose ... delight is in the law of the Lord, and in His law he meditates day and night. He shall be like a tree planted by the rivers of water, that brings forth its fruit in its season, whose leaf also shall not wither; and whatever he does shall prosper" (Ps. 1:1—3). Again, it refers to the one who receives joy in obeying God's principles, even pondering them in his spare time. His needs will remain amply provided for, and all he seeks to achieve will flourish. *Whatever* he does will succeed.

While King Hezekiah sought the Lord, we are told he upheld his commandments. Because of Hezekiah's loyalty, the Bible affirms God was with him and he thrived wherever he went. The one who fears God will accomplish what he sets his mind toward.

King David promised his son, Solomon, who would rule after him, that he would prosper if he fulfilled the commands of the Lord. David understood this universal, spiritual law. He knew prosperity was conditional. *If* he feared and obeyed God, *then* he would enjoy success. *We must prove ourselves first.*

As King David neared the end of his life, he commanded Solomon to, "keep the charge of the Lord your God: to walk in His ways, to keep His statutes, His commandments, His judgments, and His testimonies ... that you may prosper in all that you do and wherever you turn" (1 Kings 2:3). Imagine if we demanded the same of our own leaders!

Joshua assumed the leadership role of Israel upon the death of Moses, and God encouraged him to be strong and courageous. "Observe to do according to all that is written in it (the Scriptures)," God directed. "For then you will make your way prosperous, and then you will have good success ... do not be afraid, nor be dismayed, for the Lord your God is with you wherever you go" (Josh. 1:8, 9). That was a promise to Joshua thousands of years ago, and it remains for the man who follows God today. That is the beauty of God's Word. It endures, quietly awaiting the soul willing to observe and conform to its precepts.

RENEWED PURPOSE

I can scarcely fathom the instant an atheist passes away and suddenly stands in the presence of God. After a lifetime of rejecting God and his salvation provision, what flashes through his mind in that initial second? Upon this startling revelation, he would undoubtedly gasp, *"There is ... a God!"* Collapsing at the feet of his Creator, in anguish he would weep uncontrollably. I can imagine no other realistic response. The remorse and burden of guilt and shame would prove too heavy to bear.

Then consider the soul who lives his life convinced he knows God, when in truth, he simply attended church religiously. Perhaps he recited a prayer one day a friend confirmed would reserve a place for him in heaven. His fateful day arrives and he at once meets his Maker. "I do not know you," God affirms. "But I went to church every week," the man frantically replies. "I said the prayer!" The voice of God remains loving, but steadfast, "I called you, but you never came. You must now depart." Horror and terror strangle his soul as the eternal weight of spurning the Lord floods his spirit.

According to James, "The prayer of a righteous person is powerful and effective" (Jas. 5:16, NIV).[6] From this verse and others, we can rightly surmise the opposite is also true, that the prayer of an unrighteous individual is both weak and ineffective. In fact, the Bible says, "The Lord is far from the wicked, but He hears the prayer of the righteous" (Prov. 15:29, NKJV).

There are some, though assuredly a minority, who honestly believe they have never sinned in their life. It takes but a moment, a simple question or two, to expose the truth that they, in fact, have sinned innumerable times. The problem generally hinges on a common misconception of what defines sin. And while the rest of the population, meanwhile, readily admits they have sinned, the majority fail to recognize the need for someone to pay the penalty for these sins.

The remaining few who acknowledge their sin and incidental need for a Savior, are met with a real danger. Upon confessing their infractions, some feel they rarely sin anymore, or at least, nothing severe. They proudly refrain from murder, theft, and drug trafficking. But if we are truthful, these sins prove almost effortless to skirt. These individuals lose sight of the wealth of elusive sins teeming within them daily.

Arrogance, lust, coveting, bitterness, anger, and jealousy are only a few of the more latent transgressions of the heart unobserved by the public eye. Even if a person successfully identifies these wrongful conducts in his own life, he often dismisses them as he observes the behavior of another and judges them as comparably worse. "At least I am not like *that* guy," he surmises. Otherwise, he grows numb and tolerant of his misbehavior by justifying it in the name of common culture acceptance. "Premarital sex is acceptable now since everyone else is doing it," he pacifies his conscience, while suppressing the still, soft voice within.

If only he understood the faithfulness God was challenging him to pursue. If only he recognized the voice of God spurring him on toward a much richer and fuller manner of life. If only he possessed a real fear of the Lord and passion to walk according to his ways— *without compromise*. What a vastly different life he would boast!

When once a man falls in love with God, his perspective is altered and his desires are no longer the same. We are told if we know God, we will honor him and hold fast his commandments. Solomon counsels that if "you receive my words, and treasure my commands ... cry out for discernment, and lift up your voice for understanding," that person "will understand the fear of the Lord, and find the knowledge of God" (Prov. 2:1—5). A renewed purpose awakens and begins to well up within the one uniquely called a child of God.

I ponder how my life might appear today had I decided at a younger age to wholly commit myself to God. How might my life look if I determined to fully obey God *today*?

Do I desire to seek God without reservation and regardless of outcome? Am I willing to surrender my wants completely for the will of God, even if it means never getting married, never becoming wealthy, being overlooked for a promotion, receiving ridicule, or looking like a fool?

When circumstances are going well, we tend to be more prone to compromise. But as we descend into dire straits, we find ourselves willing to obey God more readily. The degree of our predicament influences our faithfulness toward God. If a person is drowning, his commitment level to God is presently all-encompassing and unwavering. He would follow God no matter what he called him to do. Just get me through this! If an individual grows gravely ill, he is moved with sincere allegiance to God. As time advances and conditions improve, the perceived need for God sadly diminishes, with loyalty shadowing closely behind.

FUNDAMENTAL PURPOSE

What God requires is no mystery. It is not a cryptic plan we must decipher or grapple over throughout the course of our lifetime to grasp. His purpose for our lives is neither complex nor confusing, but plainly revealed to us in his Word. We have only to accept or reject it.

We were *fundamentally* created for the glory of God and to mutually enjoy intimate love and fellowship with him. In order to achieve this design, however, we must turn from sin. God's will for each of our lives is our sanctification, or purification, leading to holiness, as was initially intended.

Along with our primary purpose, we are endowed with

supplemental purposes, if you will. We possess the honor of ruling over all animals, creatures, and fish of the sea. We are to care for and tend to the sphere of land in which we live. The responsibility of procreating and multiplying upon the earth are also ours to relish.

Other *complementary* purposes have developed as well, owing origins to the moment man first chose to sin. I initially wrote *fell* into sin, as is often heard, but it suddenly occurred to me how responsibility shifts from the individual, as one unwittingly falls into sin, like gravity pulling us to earth. The truth is they decidedly determined to breach the boundary set by God.

Due to the inception of sin, and the fallen nature of man ever since, we now assume other purposes with the intention of fulfilling our fundamental purpose of loving and glorifying God. We are now commissioned with the privilege of spreading the good news of forgiveness and redemption. Furthermore, we are commanded to make *disciples* of all nations, and not merely converts.

Micah explains what God requires of us: to do justly, love mercy, and humbly walk with his Lord (Micah 6:8). As God assured the Israelites, he comforts us the same. "I know the thoughts that I think toward you, says the Lord, thoughts of peace and not of evil, to give you a future and a hope" (Jer. 29:11). God continues by ensuring we will find him when we search for him with all our heart, and he will then bring us back from our captivity (Jer. 29:14). How many of us are currently suffering from some manner of captivity today, longing for restoration and liberation?

We would be wise to remember real satisfaction only comes from understanding and pursuing our fundamental purpose in life. We were created for the glory of God. He desires that we fear him by living faithfully toward him, and in so doing, enjoying him to the fullest. The Bible says, "whether you eat or drink, or whatever you do, do all to the glory of God" (1 Cor. 10:31).

Once fellowship with God is restored, we seek to know him intimately as we honor, praise, and grow in his likeness. True success stems from knowing God personally and deeply.

Points To Ponder

- The more intimately a person knows God, the more his wants will align with those of his Creator.

- As a soul genuinely seeks after God, desires will gradually transform to those which God adores.

- When once we recognize all that God has done and continues doing for us, our commitment and obedience toward him heightens.

- While the promise of prosperity is conditional, it remains a universal, spiritual law. If we fear the Lord, we shall enjoy success. But we must prove ourselves *first*.

- The Word of God endures, quietly awaiting the soul willing to observe and conform to its precepts.

- God's purpose for our lives is neither complex nor confusing, but plainly revealed in his Word. We have only to accept or reject it.

- We were fundamentally created for the glory of God, to mutually love and be loved by him, and to enjoy intimate fellowship with our Creator.

- God desires that we fear him by living faithfully toward him, and in so doing, enjoying him to the fullest. True success comes from knowing God personally and deeply.

- When a man falls in love with God, his perspective is altered and his desires are no longer the same.

THE ORACLE FOR HEALTH

Do not be wise in your own eyes;
Fear the Lord and depart from evil.
It will be health to your flesh,
and strength to your bones.
—Proverbs 3:7, 8

We all aspire a healthy quality of life. No one likes getting sick, breaking an arm, or having a stroke. Unfortunately, health problems are frequently unavoidable. As we age, our parts wear out like racking miles on a car, and eventually something gives. Ever since sin entered the world, curses have plagued this planet, from plants to animals to man. We all die. Even the healthiest and godliest man is unable to escape the inevitable.

DISOBEDIENCE FOSTERS POOR HEALTH

The causes of poor health and physical disabilities are innumerable. Oftentimes, we have no idea why certain adverse events occur. A baby is born blind, a child develops cancer, or a family perishes in an auto accident. But we may acquire comfort, for one thing is certain. Nothing happens without God's involvement or allowance, and there is nothing difficult nor beyond his control. The will of God is perfect, and even the most undesirable circumstances in our lives may be used for good to bring about his purposes. Keep in mind, though, God does not cause all things to occur, for many a person is living outside his protection. The

Word of God is clear. We risk losing his security if we turn our back on him and dwell in disobedience.

With that said, many health problems do originate in response to our depravity. There are always consequences for sin, like it or not. The cost may involve finances, reputation, threat of enemies, oppression, or compromised health. Deuteronomy pronounces a slew of curses that will inflict people who turn from God, including loss of money, plagues, sickness, wars, madness, blindness, confusion, and infidelity of a spouse. These shall not prosper, but be plundered and oppressed continually, living in recurrent need. We have but look no further than our neighbors to witness the effects of this widespread curse. If we are honest, a quick reflection of our own home will expose the consequence of sin in our personal lives.

The Israelites rebelled against the Lord, and God replied to Moses, "How long will these people reject Me? And how long will they not believe Me...? I will strike them with the pestilence and disinherit them" (Num. 14:11, 12). The people failed to fear God, but feared man instead. This is a dangerous outlook, for when we deviate from trusting God, we begin to cherish the things of the world and value the opinion of man more than God. We position ourselves beyond the protection of God, inviting a plethora of anxieties to overcome and distress us.

The Bible instructs us to "be anxious for nothing, but in everything by prayer and supplication, with thanksgiving, let your requests be made known to God" (Phil. 4:6). There is presently overwhelming evidence of the effects worry unleashes upon the human body. The drive to eat too much or too little has become routine, encouraging obesity, bulimia, or anorexia. Mild physical pains worsen, and headaches and ulcers emerge. Sleep disorders develop and depression is commonplace. If anxiety goes unchecked, in time it may trigger a stroke or heart attack. Diseases are roused, and while our quests for cures run rampant, a new illness surfaces as another is suppressed. We dwell in a depraved domain, where our disorderly behaviors continue to generate destructive effects.

Nevertheless, hope abounds. King Solomon, touted the wisest of all kings, insisted, "I surely know it will be well with those who fear God, who fear before Him. But it will not be well with the wicked" (Eccles. 8:12, 13). God desires our well-being and protection, if only we give him priority in our lives.

PROMOTING GOOD HEALTH

If sin kindles poor health, what manner should we assume when enriching our well-being? We desperately need to realign our priorities. God wants precedence. Nothing should come before him, and granted, that is easier said than done. Setting our job, possessions, personal health, or loved ones ahead of God in significance is to place an idol above him. It may not embody a physical, carved statue, but it remains an idol nonetheless. Fearing the Lord is such a monumental necessity that God established this standard as the first of the Ten Commandments. We are to possess no other gods. *This is rule number one!*

God tested the Israelites with a challenge, "If you diligently heed the voice of the Lord your God and do what is right in His sight, give ear to His commandments and keep all His statutes, I will put none of the diseases on you which I have brought on the Egyptians. For I am the Lord who heals you" (Exod. 15:26). Not only can God prompt disease, but he is the great Physician for those who are sick. As designer of our bodies, he retains the authority to produce infirmity as well as the power to cure. What an amazing God!

God reiterates his promise toward the Israelites if they will simply commit to serving him. "I will take sickness away from the midst of you. No one shall suffer miscarriage or be barren in your land; I will fulfill the number of your days. I will send My fear before you" (Exod. 23:25—27). Why does he add that last phrase regarding sending his fear before them? God is confirming his protection upon his chosen people. If they determine to honor and fear God, the Israelites would enjoy dwelling beneath his umbrella of security. The Israelite enemies would fear them because of the defense awarded by God.

The fear of the Lord, commonly regarded in a negative light, is sorely misunderstood. To fear God is by no means a harsh and dreaded notion, and if it is, our perception is gravely polluted. For the fear of the Lord is nothing less than liberating! God wants desperately to free us from the bondage of sin, which has embedded its roots too deeply to fully grasp. He seeks to refine us that we might walk in purity, and in so doing, receive blessing. What a welcoming resolve to place our fear in God. Why do we resist such divine deliverance?

When once this newfound freedom is discovered, a joy unfamiliar is unearthed. This joy is otherworldly, of foreign origins, and unattainable in this physical realm apart from God. I can almost hear the scoffing now. These plainly and regrettably have yet to experience the mercies of God.

The Bible tells us, "A merry heart does good, like medicine, but a broken spirit dries the bones" (Prov. 17:22). A joyful soul brings healing to a physical body! An individual may still die, mind you, though she is bursting with happiness. For we all must pass at some point, and we need to remember these are foundational principles, not wishes we can impose on demand. Similarly, we are told, "A sound heart is life to the body, but envy is rottenness to the bones" (Prov. 14:30). While sin may result in bitter consequences to one's health, a virtuous spirit encourages vigor to one's well-being.

Worry is iniquity, as we neglect to trust God and his provision. Even if the outcome seems unfavorable, we should dwell in the confidence that God's purpose for our lives is best. Yes, his plans are indeed better than our own. And with anxiety, as with all sin, comes a consequence, be it lack of sleep, high blood pressure, or something worse. The Proverbs caution, "Anxiety in the heart of man causes depression, but a good word makes it glad"

(Prov. 12:25). A hope built upon faith in God is medicinal to the mind and body. The state of one's spirit bears a direct impact on the condition of one's physical body. God wants us to discover freedom as we place our complete trust in his sovereignty.

Like the comfort one acquires in trusting God, kind and wise words also possess the power to strengthen one's health as the mind is calmed and appeased. The Bible says, "Pleasant words are like a honeycomb, sweetness to the soul and health to the bones" (Prov. 16:24). Likewise, "the tongue of the wise promotes health" (Prov. 12:18). A healthy mind filled with wisdom is associated with encouraging wellness in others. Joy, in the absence of anxiety, is a remarkable remedy for many a malady.

> Fear the Lord and depart from evil.
> It will be health to your flesh,
> and strength to your bones.
> —Proverbs 3:7, 8

Longevity Of Life

The majority of us would agree that long life is considered a blessing. The Scriptures attest to this viewpoint again and again, and lay out a universal principle to help ensure we endure to receive this gift. But even so, there are many good, even godly people, who die at a relatively youthful age, and still countless of innocent children who likewise perish before they are even offered a chance to rebel. These we must ultimately entrust to God, for his ways are pure and his will is perfect.

We must learn to offer God praise amidst difficult times as well as pleasant. It is almost effortless to thank God when things are progressing smoothly, when everything is going our way. It is amidst the tough circumstances when our gratefulness shines forth and God receives a much nobler glory and honor.

We may not understand why a dreadful situation occurs.

Oftentimes, the reasons are revealed months or years later, and the divine plan of God is witnessed unfolding in our lives in ways that before were unfathomable. Unfortunately, there are other times when the reasons are never unveiled, and our trust is put to the test. We can fold and shake our fist before God in bitterness and anger, or we may place our faith in the omniscience of God and allow his peace to penetrate our hearts like nothing else ever will.

The general principle on the longevity of life is uncomplicated. "The fear of the Lord prolongs days, but the years of the wicked will be shortened" (Prov. 10:27). Neither ambiguous nor complex, its sentiment is graciously sprinkled throughout Scripture. Through Moses, God admonishes us to keep his commandments that we may prolong our days (Deut. 11:8, 9).

I do not believe it could be any clearer. If we fear the one who gave us breath, there is a better chance of living longer than if we live immorally and defy God. As mentioned earlier, this is not always the case. Wicked men often live long lives, while devout men pass prematurely. God has his reasons and we may not be privileged to realize them. But the general rule persists. If we walk with God and obey his precepts, we will live longer.

The Bible says, "The fear of the Lord is the beginning of wisdom, and the knowledge of the Holy One is understanding. For by me your days will be multiplied, and years of life will be added to you" (Prov. 9:10, 11). By wisdom, the span of our lives is lengthened! Where, then, might we find and consume this revitalizing wisdom? It springs not from a distinguished intellect. Genuine wisdom is not acquired from this physical world.

Wisdom is otherworldly. God is the giver of wisdom, and he offers it liberally to all who seek it. As stated, the beginning of wisdom is the fear of the Lord. This indeed is where most individuals lose interest, for the supposed stakes are too high. The wall of self erects a grandiose obstruction. If we hold neither reverence nor awe for God, and we have no respect for his ways, we have yet to begin to gain in wisdom.

CONDITIONAL PROMISE

The promise of an extended life is a *conditional* promise. We are required to do something in order to receive the benefit of the pledge. By way of dream, the Lord spoke to King Solomon, "if you walk in My ways, to keep My statutes and My commandments, as your father David walked, then I will lengthen your days" (1 Kings 3:14). *If* you do this, *then* I will do that. We must first meet the conditions of God.

King Hezekiah was keen to this principle, though he never demanded of God the outcome he desired. When he became ill and near the point of death, Hezekiah prayed, "'Remember now, O Lord, I pray, how I have walked before You in truth and with a loyal heart, and have done what was good in Your sight.' And Hezekiah wept bitterly" (2 Kings 20:3). He lived a godly lifestyle, and so humbly pleaded for mercy.

The reply of God is amazing! "I have heard your prayer, I have seen your tears; surely I will heal you … and I will add to your days fifteen years" (2 Kings 20:5, 6). God not only hears the prayers of the righteous, but he honors their prayers. He may not always respond in the manner we hope for, but he will answer those who honor him in the way he deems best.

CONTINUAL PROMISE

Moses warned the Israelites to "fear the Lord your God, to keep all His statutes and His commandments which I command you, you and your son and your grandson, all the days of your life, and that your days may be prolonged" (Deut. 6:2). Not only is longevity conditional, contingent upon obedience, but it also remains a *continual* promise. The "you and your son and your grandson" implies the permanence of this declaration to future generations, as long as they uphold their end of the deal. God has revealed to us in this verse the very secret to life. He follows up later by stating that this is "not a futile thing for you, because it is your life" (Deut. 32:47).

The sobering words of God should awaken the one who dismisses his regard for righteousness, or the one who cavalierly holds that consequence fails to follow an action. "How long will these people reject Me?" the Lord asked Moses. "And how long will they not believe Me? I will strike them with the pestilence and disinherit them" (Num. 14:11, 12). The penalty for rejecting God serves a double-edged purpose. While unleashing discipline to the one in rebellion, it serves a merciful instrument in hopefully drawing the transgressor toward necessary repentance.

But notice how God delights in blessing without having to discipline. The heartfelt passion of God for our faithfulness and his subsequent favor upon his children is unmistakable. "Oh, that they had such a heart in them that they would fear Me and always keep all My commandments, that it might be well with them and with their children forever! You shall walk in all the ways which the Lord your God has commanded you, that you may live and that it may be well with you, and that you may prolong your days in the land which you shall possess" (Deut. 5:29, 33).

God extends the same offer to us today as he did thousands of years prior. This should arouse us with inspiration and encourage us to yield to the will of God. In so doing, he will smile upon the faithful soul and align him toward prosperity. God assures it will be well with the one who does "what is right and good in the sight of the Lord" (Deut. 6:18).

God even pledges well-being and long life to the one who honors his father and mother, "that your days may be long, and that it may be well with you" (Deut. 5:16). This consistency is apparent in light of the initial commands of God found within the Ten Commandments, and shadows a similar thread of honoring God the Father.

Regardless of how much we fear the Lord and abide in him, though, we have not the leisure of disregarding personal responsibility in maintaining our well-being. We cannot throw caution out the window to live recklessly, and trust that God will continue to uphold his part in granting us a thriving welfare. Sensible living, paired with a God-revered relationship, will invariably result in our Creator honoring us. And whom better to be honored by?

- God's will is perfect, and even the most undesirable circumstances in our lives may be used for good to bring about his purposes.

- There are always consequences for sin, sometimes resulting in compromised health.

- As we deviate from trusting in God, we begin to cherish the things of the world and value the opinion of man more than God.

- While living in sin, we risk positioning ourselves outside the protection of God, inviting a plethora of anxieties to overcome and distress us.

- We dwell in a depraved domain, where our disorderly behaviors will continue to generate destructive effects.

- God wants priority in our lives. Setting anything in significance before God is to place an idol above him.

- As designer of our bodies, God retains both the authority to produce infirmity as well as the power to heal.

- The fear of the Lord is nothing less than liberating, as God frees us from the bondage of sin.

- The state of one's spirit bears a direct impact on the condition of one's physical body.

THE ORACLE FOR WEALTH

Blessed is the man who fears the Lord ...
Wealth and riches will be in his house.
—Psalm 112:1, 3

ALLIANCE WITH WISDOM

The promises for wealth to the one who fears God are richly rooted within the Scriptures. In a world obsessed with amassing possessions and rivaling his neighbor, these pledges are impossible to avoid when exploring the Word of God. We all hope for God's favor, but how many are willing to do what it takes to warrant his approval? "May God bless you and this country" are empty words if we live contrary to his morals. We must not forget, the promises for wealth are *conditional*, based upon behavior and heart intent.

To fear the Lord is to love virtue and hate wickedness. Personified in the book of Proverbs, we are told wisdom travels in the path of uprightness that it "may cause those who love me to inherit wealth." We are also enlightened on how to gain the favor of God. "Riches and honor are with me," reveals Wisdom, and "whoever finds me finds life, and obtains favor from the Lord" (Prov. 8:35). The intensity of man's fear of the Lord and the depth of his wisdom are brilliantly intertwined and inseparable. The greater the fear of God perceived, the more profound the wisdom grasped.

The Blessing Of Riches

The promises of prosperity are general principles, whereby the observer is often awarded. But God may never be viewed as one who *must* provide wealth when once we choose obedience. Blessed we will be, but not always with riches. God is far more concerned with our spiritual condition than our physical or financial state of being. In fact, the physical and tangible is oftentimes forfeited for the advancement of the spiritual. And though an individual may prove faithful toward God, he may well decide to call the believer home rather than rain wealth upon his head for faultless reasons only he may be privy. One godly man enjoys a life of financial plenitude, while another virtuous man struggles to make ends meet. We must love God and trust him to carry out his plan for our lives, regardless of outcome.

We are told God appoints both the poor and the rich. God moves some to lower depths, while others he exalts (1 Sam. 2:7). For this reason, we can rest assure God has our best interest in mind, even when it seems blessing evades us. Sometimes unfavorable events occur. That may very well be a part of his sovereign plan, at least at that specific time in our life. He may be testing our heart or placing us in a trial to further develop character. But to shake our fist at God when apparent blessing is withheld only affirms our misguided grounds for compliance to the standards of God.

That said, the promises of prosperity remain universal principles nonetheless. Proverbs teaches that "by humility and the fear of the Lord are riches and honor and life" (Prov. 22:4). As our fear of God matures, humility follows. Aligning God in the center of our lives enlightens our perspective as we recognize that apart from him we are empty and destitute.

King Solomon tells us "for every man to whom God has given riches and wealth, and given him power to eat of it, to receive his heritage and rejoice in his labor—this is the gift of God" (Eccles. 5:19). Wealth can be a gift when used appropriately according to the will of God. Abused or adored, money can quickly become a curse. But it need not, when possessions are surrendered over to God to be used as he determines and leads, for "the blessing of the Lord makes one rich, and He adds no sorrow with it" (Prov. 10:22).

Is Wealth Immoral?

The wealthiest man in the world will perish as penniless as the poorest. Both shall stand before God and give an account of his life. Neither will possess money, nor would it benefit if they had. The rich man enjoys his luxuries in vain if he chooses to live for himself rather than God. He literally lives at his own expense.

The Word of God warns against forsaking the Lord when you do live in prosperity. He knows many of us will grow proud and quickly neglect him as our perceived need for him diminishes. God knows us better than we know ourselves. He often withholds blessing until we are spiritually equipped and mature, or else he blesses in an alternate way altogether.

We must guard from reducing God to a simple equation, where a precise outcome *must* result if all elements are in place. Even if all facets of a godly life are present, this by no means guarantees monetary riches will fall into our lap. The one seeking money as his highest ambition will oft never attain it. Ironically, the one pursuing God in sincerity shall *always* discover wealth. While this frequently includes material possessions, for the moral laws of God favor the compliant soul, sometimes it consists of grander treasures still, perhaps the loftiest of tasting God more deeply. Remember, God chooses whom and in what manner to prosper. So regardless of the blessing to unfold, for one assuredly will, consider the following proverb.

> Better is a little with the fear of the Lord,
> than great treasure with trouble.
> —Proverbs 15:16

There is nothing immoral about possessing wealth. God has blessed many with riches, and this makes him no less moral. So at the risk of believing obtaining award for following God is unethical, let us remember a couple of men who acquired wealth in times past for honoring him.

Jacob, one of the patriarchs of the Israelites, and later named Israel, worked for his father-in-law, Laban, many years tending his flocks of sheep. Upon receiving deceptive wages time and again, Jacob wished to move elsewhere. Laban knew God had prospered him because of his son-in-law, and pleaded with Jacob to remain. Striking an agreement, Jacob resolved to stay as long as he received a share of the profits. If Laban agreed for Jacob to keep as his wage all speckled lambs, the flocks all mysteriously bore speckled. When Laban changed Jacob's wages to include only streaked lambs, the sheep produced streaked. Wages again altered to permit merely spotted, and all flocks delivered spotted lambs. Through God's provision, Jacob prospered financially by amassing a wealth of flocks from the hand of his unjust father-in-law.

God moved with favor upon another man, King Solomon, by granting him not only the wisdom and discernment he requested, but also lavished him with riches and honor, unlike any other king in his day. The Lord added a further conditional blessing as well. If Solomon faithfully walked in the ways of God, his years of life would be lengthened.

As God at times blesses with wealth, we may reason that riches are not immoral. What we then do with said money is a different story, for the lures are many by association. We are held accountable for our stewardship upon all God places within our sphere of influence. Once possessions assume an illegitimate role in our life, it is not money but *we* who have become immoral.

We must come to grips with the reality that worldly wealth, while not necessarily bad in itself, becomes immoral in the highly esteemed pursuit. Proverbs clearly warns us against overworking to acquire riches. Because wealth is so short-lived, it entreats us to stop. "For riches certainly make themselves wings; they fly away like an eagle toward heaven" (Prov. 23:4, 5).

We are continually tempted to envy those around us and compete with others more affluent. We need to remember this also is sin, and instead, we ought align ourselves with a proper perspective. We are told the rich man takes nothing with him when he dies, and so his glory fades the same. How foolish to make material abundance our life-long pursuit!

This eminent pursuit is key. Again, there is nothing wrong with working hard and striving to support and provide for a family. These are admirable qualities. But when the priorities in life become unbalanced and wealth receives a higher honor than God intended, trouble surfaces. Matthew cautions against seeking "treasures on earth, where moth and rust destroy and where thieves break in and steal; but lay up for yourselves treasures in heaven, where neither moth nor rust destroys and where thieves do not break in and steal. For where your treasure is, there your heart will be also" (Matt. 6:19).

A common notion resonates time and again. As we center our hearts with God instead of other wants, we gain twofold. We not only experience God more intimately, but we also receive the desires of our hearts. Often, when someone passionately seeks a spouse, they have a frustrating time in doing so until they align that priority into its proper abode. The same is true with finances and other areas of life. As we seek God first, while entrusting our desires with him, we discover our needs and wants are met, frequently more substantially than we could have otherwise imagined.

WARNINGS FOR WEALTH SEEKERS

The primary problem with seeking money so vehemently is that it exalts possessions to a loftier position than God. Wealth, financial security, and the quest thereof become literal gods. While not tangible, graven images, they are no less idols adored and revered. The first commandment is tossed aside as we forsake the fear of the Lord. There is no skirting the issue: *Worshiping anything but God invites bitter consequence.*

Proverbs warns the man who hurries to gain wealth will not go unpunished. "A man with an evil eye hastens after riches, and does not consider that poverty will come upon him" (Prov. 28:20, 22). Job further admonishes, "If I have made gold my hope, or said to fine gold, 'You are my confidence' … this also would be an iniquity deserving of judgment, for I would have denied God who is above" (Job 31:24, 28).

We are cautioned that the love of money is a root of all sorts of evil. Wealth in and of itself is not wicked, and yet the *love* of riches is indeed. Men in pursuit of money provoke envy and temptation, some even wandering "from the faith in their greediness, and pierced themselves through with many sorrows" (1 Tim. 6:9, 10).

On the contrary, a faithful man is promised abounding blessings. "He who trusts in his riches will fall, but the righteous will flourish like foliage" (Prov. 11:28). The righteous will flourish like foliage! Images of wellness, increase, joy, and unrestrained growth spring forth. A ravishing portrayal of prosperity is depicted. If wealth increases, we do well to never set our heart upon it (Ps. 62:10).

I ponder the predictable ascent and descent of a person's perceived need for God, and the rich and famous come to mind. What a surprising disadvantage this "fortunate" state of man bears. He considers himself self-sufficient, in need of little. He buys what he wants and people admire him, usually for the simple fact that he is rich and famous. He discerns no need for a Savior. How unfortunately accurate is the parable of a camel more comfortably walking through the eye of a needle than a man of wealth entering the kingdom of God.

THE TITHE

I am a strong advocate of the tithe. I hear a groan already. Originating in the Old Testament, God mandated ten percent of one's income as an offering to him. This would include the first fruits of an individual's revenue—not the *last* fruits, mind you, or ten percent of whatever might remain after everything else was accounted for or purchased. Otherwise, a person could easily rationalize initially paying his mortgage, utilities, phone bill, cable, internet, insurance, repairs, remodeling, health costs, schooling, food, car, and clothing expenses. I propose he would then justify bearing entertainment expenditures, retirement accounts, and other unexpected costs until, at last, he conveniently had nothing left to offer.

The tithe is arguably the most prudent investment a person can make. Yes, *investment*. Virtually all expenses in this world are useful toward life here on earth, whether for survival or luxury or somewhere in between. But an offering to God, when used appropriately, has the ability of impacting his kingdom for eternity. Not only do the effects and benefits transcend the confines of time, the returns on the investment can multiply for generations. Furthermore, God desires to bless those who honor him with their wealth, so it proves the soundest investment of all.

God is never short on money, so the need is not with him. Rather, the need is within man, to confirm that money owns him not, as he releases its tight grip upon his soul. As one entrusts his money to God, he discovers not only liberation in giving what one holds dear, but a privilege in watching God multiply that which he first gave us.

In Malachi, God cursed the Israelites for robbing him of the tithes and offerings they withheld. When an individual holds back what is due God, he restrains his blessing upon that person. It remains a simple principle grossly neglected. Give and it shall be given to you, and the inverse, withhold and from you it shall be withheld.

God challenges the Israelites to return what they owe, and in turn, he would "open for (them) the windows of heaven and pour out for (them) such blessing that there will not be room enough to receive it" (Mal. 3:10). God tells them to try him, or test him, to see if he would not indeed rain prosperity above that which they could even handle. "Return to me," God says, "and I will return to you." What a merciful promise, if only we repent and turn back to God!

Wait a moment, I hear murmuring in the back. The tithe, defined in the Old Testament, is found nowhere in the New Testament. Therefore, no longer under the law, we are not obligated to give a tenth. I do not bear a huge problem with that line of reasoning, as long as one is likewise content with relinquishing the "and it shall be given to you" promise in Scripture. I also have a difficult time believing God demanded a tithe before the Messiah arrived, and then changed his mind to "Oh, just give whatever you want, and if you want." The intent of the tithe still applies today.

God will not force a person to give, as it must spring from the heart, or at the least, out of obedience. I do agree we are not limited to a tenth either. If a person wants to offer twenty percent, so be it. But in taking liberty in tithing, a general tendency is to err on the lighter side, and render perhaps three percent. This may very well defeat the premise of the giving in the first place, as one offers less and less of what is expected. One flirts with the sentiment that God has not provided enough to enable him to present the amount required. While God may render the believer some margin of tolerance here, remember the blessing may coincide with the generosity conveyed.

We are no longer under the law, it is true, and yet, the elementary reason for the tithe remains. God demands that a person love him and not money, and if we are unable to part with some of it, it owns us and we become its slave. If the Old Testament commanded one to love his neighbor, but the command was absent in the New Testament, is one exempt to disregard love for his neighbor today? Heaven forbid! Reason beckons he continue to love regardless.

If we consider, too, for example, the command to observe a day of rest each week, we fail to find the same instruction in the New Testament. Again, while man is not bound by the law, this demand was given prior to sin entering the world. The principal reason for the command lingers. As with money, man must honor God with his time, not to mention, man also requires needed physical and mental rest. To dismiss commands on the basis of lack of duplicity in the New Testament, while reason supports its permanence, is simply literary legalism.

Before pressing on, I still hear a faint grumble and restlessness in the dark recesses. Oh, why does money have such affect! "I don't have money to give right now," one rebuts. "But I will definitely give when I have a surplus." First of all, larger expenses typically accompany greater wealth, so this argument may easily extend forever. One readily justifies needing just a bit more before he is able to give. Secondly, and just as importantly, if an individual cannot afford to give presently, it proves he cannot afford *not* to give immediately! This person has completely misunderstood the concept of the tithe.

Giving monetarily demonstrates an expression of thanksgiving, sacrifice, and worship. The physical act of offering a tithe is actually the outpouring of the spiritual. When given with pure intentions, it represents a reverential obedience of the heart. Everyone is able to give something today. Everyone. Give and it shall be given to you. Why would anyone hesitate, especially a person in need. Honor God and rise to his challenge to offer the tithes he requires, whatever that percentage may be. Return to God and all that is due him. The dividends God pays are far better than the money we invest. Again, view your offering as an investment, one that will never disappoint.

SEEK FIRST HIS KINGDOM

God forces no one to return to him. But he awaits with open arms, as the father with his prodigal son. When the son returned home, his father immediately ran to meet him. He was actively looking with hopeful anticipation of his return. He forgave at once his wayward son. He honored him with restored position and gifts including a ring, robe, and the killing of a calf—not just any calf—the fattened one awaiting celebration!

When all is said and done, if God wishes you financial wealth, you will attain riches. If he wills not, you will not amass wealth though you die trying. And in the case you do gain wealth against the will of the Father, for often he does allow us to go our own way, it comes with a curse. Therefore, rest in the Lord and seek first his kingdom.

Points To Ponder

- The promises for wealth are conditional, based upon our behavior and heart intent.

- The intensity of man's fear of the Lord and the depth of his wisdom are brilliantly intertwined and inseparable. The greater the fear of God perceived, the more profound the wisdom grasped.

- God is far more concerned with our spiritual condition than that of our physical state of being.

- Our perspective is enlightened as we align God in the center of our lives. We learn to recognize God as our hope and our all, and apart from him, we are truly nothing.

- As we choose to seek God first, while entrusting our desires with him, we discover our needs and wants are met, frequently more substantially than we could have otherwise imagined.

- The tithe transcends the confines of time, as return on investment multiplies for generations.

- If an individual cannot afford to give presently, he cannot afford *not* to give immediately!

- Giving monetarily demonstrates an expression of thanksgiving, sacrifice, and worship. The physical act of offering a tithe is actually the outpouring of the spiritual.

The Oracle For Hope

For I know the thoughts that I think toward you,
says the Lord, thoughts of peace and not of evil,
to give you a future and a hope.
—Jeremiah 29:11

Confide In God Alone

God has a wonderful plan for each of us. If we wander another path, distinct from the Lord, troubles surface. We hear from the very mouth of God, "Cursed is the man who trusts in man and makes flesh his strength, whose heart departs from the Lord" (Jer. 17:5). If we place all confidence in ourselves, we are ultimately doomed to grief and failure. Unhappiness will be familiar and routine in our lives as we struggle to unearth joy from individuals and worldly things.

The warning is unmistakable. The one who disregards God is plagued with a curse. The curse may afflict finances, health, marriage, loved ones, or countless other facets of life. There is no avoiding the inevitable, for curses will certainly befall. It is only a matter of time.

Thankfully, there is another option and we need not live beneath the weight of a curse. God eagerly searches this world for the man or woman who might dare love him wholeheartedly. Notice the blunt contrast in God's encouraging and comforting words, "Blessed is the man who trusts in the Lord, and whose hope is the Lord" (Jer. 17:7).

Hope Of The Righteous

Life is short, brutally short. As a child, our life ahead seems end-less, but as time passes and our bodily wear grows bitterly appar-ent, we realize the horrible brevity of it all. Generations come and go, seeking fortunes while occupying a tiny parcel of land called home. Some find wealth as others scrape by, yet in the end, both leave with nothing. Centuries become millenniums, and millions morph into billions. It is difficult to fathom the untold palette of people who have tread and been brushed off the canvas of earth. So many have lived. So many have died. And for what?

The fleeting breath of life is nothing in light of the breadth of eternity. But be not misled, for the repercussions of our faint footprints within humanity are priceless. How we live today will forever condition our future. To live merely for the present is not only vanity, it is borderline insanity, when at long last we recog-nize the implications of our behavior.

There exists a strong alliance between the righteous and the provision of God. The link binding the two is strengthened and braced by the Word of God. The Bible says, "The eyes of the Lord are on the righteous, and His ears are open to their prayers" (1 Pet. 3:12). What encouraging words for the soul struggling to live uprightly. The Creator is actively watching those who pursue him. Anyone may fall prey to iniquity, for it requires little regard to surrender to its appeal. But the one who declines the lure of sin offers the sacrifice of righteousness, and him God holds in high esteem. He protects and cares for him. He comprehends his need and hears his appeal. God dearly loves the righteous.

But woe to the man who is friend of sin! The remaining part of the prior verse plainly warns us, "the face of the Lord is against those who do evil" (1 Pet. 3:12). Just as God moves on behalf of the godly, he frustrates and provokes the ways of the unrighteous. When man discovers God working against him, it matters not how much he strives. His desperate pursuits are fruitless. The Bible tells us the hand of God is in favor of the one who loves him, but "His power and His wrath are against all those who forsake Him" (Ezra 8:22). How equally magnificent to rest in the arms of God for well-being, and dreadfully horrific to taste of his fury.

Once more, the love of God is compared to the earthly father toward his child. David explains that as great a height the heavens are beyond the earth, so vast is the mercy of God with those who fear him. As a father shows sympathy to his children, so the Lord is compassionate toward the one who fears him (Ps. 103:11, 13).

Proverbs inspires us to "be zealous for the fear of the Lord all the day; for surely there is a hereafter, and your hope will not be cut off" (Prov. 23:17, 18). The word *zealous* expresses a strong eagerness and passion to fear God. We find our hope in the Lord. Everything else will disappoint and fail to furnish the fulfillment in life we crave. All other hope is counterfeit.

The Faithful Few

The Israelites witnessed firsthand the deliverance of God from the hand of the Egyptians, observing plague after plague, until they were liberated. They beheld the parting of the Red Sea, and walked across dry land before watching their enemies drown as the waters crashed upon them. Yet even after such wonders, they refused to heed the voice of God—except for one man.

Caleb had a different spirit within him, we are told, one committed to fully following God. For this reason, God vowed to bring him into the land of blessing (Num. 14:23, 24). All others would die before entering this Promised Land. But Caleb held a special place in God's heart for his unwavering obedience. Caleb was far from perfect. God understands our humanity better than ourselves, and he knows we will stumble. But the heart of Caleb was loyal to God.

God is actively looking for the faithful few amidst a darkened world of compromising souls. He longs to reward the man or woman possessing faith to step out and hold his name in high regard.

Challenging times will arise, even for the upright. But the Lord promises to remain by our side and sustain us. He will serve as our front guide and rear guard, providing direction and protection (Isa. 52:12). Many prefer to travel alone, and they encounter a life congested with frenzied forks and obscure alleys. Not so with the righteous. So secure is the course in life with God at the helm, we are told their way is a highway (Prov. 15:19). Images of straight, spacious lanes with shoulders spring to mind. The godly man reclines comfortably with his Lord, enjoying a scenic drive with an overwhelming sensation of peace, while admiring the open sky and expanse ahead.

His life is by no means flawless, but he remains calm and content, with little regret. When he passes through deep waters, for assuredly he will, God will never leave him nor allow him to be swept over. And though he walks through fire, he will never burn (Isa. 43:2).

Fellowship Restored

How do I acquire this hope amidst a seemingly hopeless world? We can attend church regularly, donate money to charity, and volunteer time for commendable causes. We can reserve time for daily prayer and Scripture reading, take up fasting, and sing hymns until we are blue in the face. While these are all worthy pursuits, they are performed in vain unless the heart is first transformed.

We may render a portion of our heart and preserve our present lifestyle, while offering God the opportunity to ride alongside. But hope is forfeited for the right to live as we very well please. A personal change must take place.

God stands ready to pardon our sins and relent from causing harm. He is quick to forgive, wishing to restore his children. But we must *first* return to him with sincerity (Joel 2:12, 13). Joel pleads for us to rend, or tear, our hearts instead of our clothing. Forget about external actions initially. Focus instead on the inward, secret recesses of the mind. Submit to God, and outward behavior will change—not the other way around.

But why must we return *first*? Why does God not forgive us, bless us, and then await our return? For one, we likely would never return. And secondly, God *did* respond first. While we were inundated with sin, he died for us! What more could he do? It now falls on each of us to act, to humbly fall on our face and admit our immorality and resistance toward God.

Seizing all of our sins, God will toss them into the sea, remembering them no more (Mic. 7:19). God rejoices over each and every soul who comes to him in repentance, and how ironic is the joy of the Lord, as we are the ones who so desperately need him. The prophet Jeremiah advised the people of Jerusalem and Judah that if they turned from their wicked ways and obeyed God, he would relent of the destruction he had already declared against them (Jer. 26:13). He was inclined to change his mind if they were willing to pursue him.

We possess the same opportunity today. Has God pronounced doom on you for living your life as you determine, with disregard for his morals? Has he sent confusion or affliction that never seems to cease? Are you lacking peace or clinging to false hope, that perhaps the circumstances in your life are completely isolated and unrelated to the influence of God?

God wants his people to stand out from the rest of the world as attractively different. Our sanctification is his aim, requiring the purging of sin and purification of our mind. God calls us to sanctify the Lord in our hearts, and with fear and humility, stand ready to explain to anyone who wonders of the hope that dwells in us (1 Pet. 3:13).

Be separate from the world, and God will walk and dwell among you (2 Cor. 6:16). How remarkable a concept. We need only to step out in faith and personalize it.

FUTURE OUTLOOK

Solomon explains in Ecclesiastes that there is a time for every-thing, a season for joy, sorrow, life, and death. How comforting to place our trust in the hands of the one who instilled in us life, who died in our place that we might live forever with him.

Peter says whoever fears God and lives righteously is looked upon with favor (Acts 10:35). God comforted Moses by promising his presence would accompany him, and he would bless him with rest (Exod. 33:14). With so much anxiety in the world, why would anyone resist lending their cares and worries over to the manage-ment of God? Moses advised the Israelites to set themselves apart for the Lord that they might receive a blessing (Exod. 32:29).

The Psalms exhort us to fear the Lord, and he will satisfy our desires and save us when we cry out to him (Ps. 145:19). We are assured the righteous who fear God will not lack anything good (Ps. 34:10).

From where does your hope spring? Even amidst persecution, Jesus encourages us to not only rejoice, but be *exceedingly* happy, for your reward in heaven will be great (Matt. 5:12). Jesus further challenges us toward great faith by affirming anything is possible if only we believe (Mark 9:23). Talk about hope! Regardless of present circumstance, the prospects are limitless for the one who repents and alters his way.

The author of Psalm 130 reveals his hope is found in the Word of God (Ps. 130:5). Scripture is full of promise to the person who heeds its instruction, and it is up to each of us to determine whether or not we will confide in its doctrine. I love how God confirms his authority. He affirms, "I am the Lord. I speak, and the word which I speak will come to pass" (Ezek. 12:25).

The apostle Paul tells us godliness is advantageous toward ev-erything, and holds promise of both this life and of that to come. He adds, "this is a faithful saying and worthy of all acceptance" (1 Tim. 4:8, 9).

God admonishes his people to listen, obey, and pursue him. If indeed a person will, he tells him to "open your mouth wide, and I will fill it" (Ps. 81:10). Hope abounds for the individual who surrenders to God his life!

Points To Ponder

- The individual who disregards God is plagued with a curse.

- The repercussions of our faint footprints within humanity will forever condition our future.

- There exists a strong alliance between the righteous and the provision of God.

- As God moves on behalf of the godly, he frustrates and provokes the ways of the unrighteous.

- God longs to reward the person possessing faith to step out and hold his name in high regard.

- Hope is forfeited for the right to live as we very well please.

- Submit to God, and outward behavior will change...not the other way around.

- God wants to bless his people today, as he did thousands of years ago, but only if they return to him first.

- Our sanctification is God's aim, requiring the purging of sin and purification of our mind.

- Regardless of present circumstance, the prospects are limitless for the one who repents and alters his way.

THE ORACLE FOR JOY

God gives wisdom and knowledge and joy
to a man who is good in His sight.
—Ecclesiastes 2:26

JOY COMES FROM THE LORD

The preceding verse reveals that joy, amongst other attributes, is granted by God. He searches for the good man or woman to bless. Yet the Bible is clear none in this world are righteous. So who then is considered *good*? Who may attain the approval of God with such lofty standards as only a holy Being upholds?

If we continue reading the remainder of the verse above, we learn while God gives joy to the good man, the joy of the sinner is oppressed. Then who may be joyful, for all have sinned but one? The answer, I submit, is two-fold. First and foremost, a person must place his trust in the one who knew no sin. Only those who embrace Jesus' offer of forgiveness and exoneration are deemed cleansed by his blood. Those who reject his provision remain tarnished in iniquity.

Secondly, while the believer enjoys the assurance of salvation, his sins nevertheless continue to bear consequence. Hence, the child of God who persists in sin will himself discover a deficiency in joy. I believe the good man blessed with joy is the individual who believes in the redemption of Jesus, while walking obediently in the manner of God.

King David assures us completeness in joy is found in God,

and everlasting pleasures are at his right hand (Ps. 16:11). He heals the sorrowful, the joyless, and the brokenhearted. God liberates the oppressed and frees the sinner from the bondage of sin that continually suppresses.

We learn that joy is unveiled to those who trust in the Lord. Proverbs attests happy is he who keeps the ways of God (Prov. 29:18), and to him who extends mercy to those in need (Prov. 14:21).

You have undoubtedly known or witnessed a wealthy individual who lacked joy. Perhaps he was bitter, jealous, lonely, full of regret, resentment, or burdened with guilt. Regardless of measure of money and accumulated possessions, he can never seem to attain lasting happiness. Satisfaction in riches is a facade.

There are conditions in this life which allude to happiness, but a genuine, deep-seeded joy comes only from God. The joy of the Lord flourishes regardless of present circumstance.

GOD FULFILLS THE DESIRE OF THE RIGHTEOUS

Life is full of choices. We decide daily how to spend our time, money, talents, and thoughts. These decisions, in turn, define priorities and paint a picture of our personality and character. Numerous things throughout the day demand our attention and insist on securing precedence. But do not be swindled!

God must possess first place in our lives if we endeavor to experience a life of prosperity. Second place is never good enough, for no idol shall be placed above him. God wants us to love him *wholeheartedly*. He enlightens us again and again that the one who loves him is the one who is obedient. The Bible assures the man who delights in the commandments of God and fears him will be blessed (Ps. 112:1).

Blessed how? David tells us, "the Lord preserves all who love Him, but all the wicked He will destroy" (Ps. 145:20). He protects and sustains the one who abides in him. We are promised God "will fulfill the desire of those who fear Him; He also will hear their cry and save them" (Ps. 145:19). What a wonderful assurance! The Creator will hear our plea and rescue us.

But there is more. God will satisfy our *desires*. He knows us better than we know ourselves. He understands the needs and inner yearnings of our soul. Interestingly, the one who fears the Lord will naturally choose to walk in obedience, and thus, bear more appropriate desires. As we develop an intimate relationship with God, these properly aligned desires will embody longings we were created to enjoy that God alone is able to fulfill. King David tells us God "satisfies the longing soul, and fills the hungry soul with goodness" (Ps. 107:7).

David also pleads with us to fear the Lord, for "there is no want to those who fear Him ... those who seek the Lord shall not lack any good thing" (Ps. 34:10). The sons of Korah concur, "no good thing will He withhold from those who walk uprightly" (Ps. 84:11). Notice they do not promise God will provide anything and everything a person wants. Oftentimes, our desires are ill-conceived and rather detrimental to us were we to receive them. God protects those he loves by withholding things he recognizes as damaging, and mercifully chooses at times not to give. While awarding a son ten million dollars at the age of thirteen may sound wonderful to the child, it almost certainly will prove disastrous. Until the youngster can prove himself a wise steward of wealth and display ample maturity and discernment, a sizable sum of money must be withheld. God moves similarly, often denying petitions from a spirit of love and protection.

> Delight yourself also in the Lord,
> and He shall give you the desires of your heart.
> —Psalm 37:4

Loving God should be neither agonizing nor dreadful—anything but. If so, there is something profoundly amiss. I submit it stems from a misunderstanding of all God has done for us, and the depth of forgiveness and reconciliation he offers.

Loving God should literally be a delight to the believer with proper understanding. Fearing God through obedience should be a joy as one gives gratitude for such a compassionate Creator. If we hold these attitudes, David assures we will receive the desires of our heart. Notice he does not say that he might give, he will probably give, or he will most likely give your desires. He *shall* give them to you. This is a promise. Granted, it is a conditional promise based on our behavior. So for heaven's sake, fulfill the conditions and claim this promise! Do not wait for some future event or further prodding. Meditate on this if you must, but alter your mind and *radically* commit yourself to God.

PREVAILING PEACE

The soul who fears the Lord will unleash a peace that transcends the world's understanding. It is a peace completely foreign to this world, originating from an infinite God rather than self. Those who love God and righteousness possess assurance they can accomplish or undergo anything with the abiding presence of Christ. Nothing may hinder them unless the purpose of God permit it so. The conscience will savor a serene state of mind deficient of worry that King Solomon ensures their sleep will be sweet, void of anxiety or fear of trouble (Prov. 3:24).

Amidst periods of uncertainty, God serves as guide. He promises to direct our path if we set our trust in him. Acknowledge him in all things and commit to living uprightly. Even during troublesome times and surrounded by a world of chaos, peace prevails, for God prevails and his rule endures.

The words of Peter resound with tranquility, "If anyone suffers as a Christian, let him not be ashamed, but let him glorify God in this matter" (1 Pet. 4:16). Certainly the world will be watching, attempting to interpret the peace a follower of Christ humbly boasts while suffering affliction or persecution. The world will stand puzzled with intrigue.

A PROPER RELATION

Joy is often confused with the notion of happiness. Happiness is generally a shallow and surface emotion. The feeling comes and goes on the basis of present conditions. If a person enjoys a pleasant night of uninterrupted sleep, or it happens to be an especially gorgeous sunny day, or one suddenly finds himself the owner of a new car, the euphoria of happiness erupts. Unfortunately, a poor night's rest befalls, sunny days lose their splendor with the onslaught of a storm, and dings and rust befriend new vehicles. Happiness can be terribly short-lived.

True happiness, or joy, lies in a proper relation between a person and his Creator. "Blessed is *every* one who fears the Lord, who walks in His ways ... you *shall* be happy, and it *shall* be well with you" (Ps. 128:1, 2). Could he be any more straightforward? Fear God. Live morally upright. *This is the secret to an abundant life!*

In fearing the Lord, a person will invariably live righteously. So in order to receive joy, blessing, and prosperity, one simply needs to commit to observing two short words. *Fear God.* This alone is the simple and pure message of the Oracle which prevailed long before this world was ever conceived. Who will stand from the crowd and heed this divine directive? Who will pursue without restraint this life aim and purpose? Who will decide to live radically and commit their ways to honoring God no matter what?

Regardless of current circumstance, joy abides in the one who recognizes from whom it springs. God is the giver of lasting joy, even in the face of adversity and sorrow. Challenging times for everyone will develop, for certain. Jesus tells us tribulation will abound in this world, but to remain joyful, for he has overcome the world (John 16:33). The peace of God transcends finite understanding, and yet, proves abundantly real to the man who retains it.

Our confidence lies in God. Without him, life is hollow and vain. The Bible says the anticipation of the wicked will die, but the hope of the blameless is gladness (Prov. 10:28). David's hope is apparent as he speaks to God: "In Your presence is fullness of joy; at Your right hand are pleasures forevermore" (Ps. 16:11).

What is possibly even more amazing is the joy *God* receives as we pursue him. God places his fear in the heart of man for the purpose of keeping him from going astray. As we live in accordance to the ways of God, he delights over us. The Bible tells us God actually *receives* pleasure from those who fear him in love and adoration (Ps. 147:11). And at the risk of being taken lightly, we are told he does so with all his heart and soul (Jer. 32:40, 41). What astonishing assurance that God yearns to prosper us!

Jesus promises, "if you abide in Me, and My words abide in you, you will ask what you desire, and it shall be done for you." He follows by conveying his love for us, and explains if a believer keeps his commandments, that person will abide in his love. Why does he tell us these things? "These things I have spoken to you, that My joy may remain in you, and that your joy may be full" (John 15:7-11).

Genuine joy springs from God. He created man to experience continual joy in his presence. He wants each believer to live a life of enduring fulfillment, and knows that any alternative without him is nothing short of hopeless.

"This is the day the Lord has made; we will rejoice and be glad in it" (Ps. 118:24). The author asserts he *will* rejoice, for joy is certainly a choice!

- In fearing the Lord, a person will invariably live righteously, and as a result, realize joy, blessing, and prosperity.

- Properly aligned desires will embody longings we were created to enjoy that God alone is able to fulfill.

- No good thing will be withheld from the one who fears God.

- If loving God is agonizing or dreadful, something is profoundly amiss. It stems from a misunderstanding of all God has done for us.

- The soul who fears the Lord will unleash a peace completely foreign to this world, originating from an infinite God rather than self.

- Real joy lay in a proper relation between a person and his Creator.

- The peace of God transcends finite understanding, and yet, proves abundantly real to the man who retains it.

- The Creator of the world longs to fulfill the desires of the creature within his creation!

- God wants man to experience enduring joy and fulfillment in his presence, and knows that any alternative without him is nothing short of hopeless.

Embracing The Oracle

Who is the man that fears the Lord?
Him shall He teach in the way He chooses.
He himself shall dwell in prosperity ...
The secret of the Lord is with those who fear Him.
—Psalm 25:12—14

Falling In Love

I was raised in an active Christian home where the teachings of Scripture were taught relentlessly. I learned to love God at an early age. He created me and sent his Son to die for me. How could I *not* love him? Nobody else had ever done that for me, and besides, I did not revel in the idea of going to hell when I perished. What a dreadful, despicable place!

It was not until I was thirty years old when I had an aha moment regarding my lack of love and commitment toward God. Through unfortunate (now recognized as fortunate) circumstances, I suddenly found myself drowning in a personal pool of despair. My world collapsed overnight as my sense of security and hope instantly vanished. An overwhelming sensation of hopelessness swallowed me as a dark cave enveloped all around. I had nowhere to turn but to God.

I lay flat, my face to the floor, and cried out to God. I never comprehended the idea of lying prostrate before God until that afternoon. I thought Biblical characters assumed the position when they had a rather eminent appeal or prayer to offer. I failed to realize the involuntary response it represented to the desperate need of a sinner when exposed to the vast gulf existing between he and a holy God. It portrayed a matter of the heart beyond the manner of posture. I suddenly understood the depth of my impurity, and the cost of the sacrifice on my behalf. The Savior of the world was literally cursed for my sake as he bore the weight of my guilt and shame.

Seeking forgiveness, and with tears streaming, I embedded my face deeper into the carpet in attempt at lowering myself but slightly further before my Creator. The half-inch depth into the dense carpet I struggled to depress painted the shame my soul endured and exchanged for restoration with a merciful God in my pursuit.

In the next few moments, I gave everything I possessed over to God. I named all things within my sphere of influence that I treasured, and released their control to the will of God. While not physically rendered, I genuinely surrendered mental ownership, for God to either take or bless my holdings as he wished. I never realized the liberation in loosening my grip and letting go of what I personally held so dear. One by one, I offered my possessions, my car, my home, my occupation, my potential future wife and children, my future itself, my health, and my life. For any who may believe this an easy task, as these things were not tangibly lost, I assure you it was an excruciating undertaking for me. I have needed to repeat this mental exercise and prayer a few times since, as my inclination is to assume authority once again. What a false sense of control I gravitate toward!

The experience is difficult to describe with words, both wonderfully freeing and gut-wrenchingly painful all the while. What a terribly agonizing day. What an amazing day, I shall never forget, as my eyes presently water in reminiscing. I had always loved him, but it was in those moments I fell *in love* with God. The nearer I now draw toward God, the greater the revelation I discern of my deeper, more latent sins, inviting an even sounder love for him.

I embraced the Oracle that day, fearing God, and submitting to his authority. Often I fail, sometimes miserably, to uphold my loyalty to God and his Word. But thankfully, he is merciful and gracious to forgive and restore with each genuine, repentant heart.

A Heart For God

How many of you can say, "I love God"? Though multitudes are able, for it has ascended an almost trendy adage to allege, these three words remain virtually hollow and meaningless. For those capable, are you then able to comfortably say with sincerity, "I love *the Lord, my God and my Savior*"? The numbers abruptly dwindle, for a personal relationship with God is unfamiliar, as he represents a superstition at worst and a distant acquaintance at best. Of this remnant, who is further able to fondly assert, "I'm *in love with* the Lord, my God and my Savior"? The stage is all but desolate now. Where did everyone go? A divine intimacy resonates with few individuals. What a profound difference that dwells with those who delight relationally to God!

I now question whether or not I love God with all my heart. My natural inclination promptly responds a resounding "yes", of course I do, for he gave me life, he died for me, he alone is my hope. But I am confident that would confirm me a liar, or at least self-deceptive. For to love the Lord wholly means to hate sin, to turn from evil and temptation at all cost, to refuse to compromise my faithfulness toward God. It has much to do with my level of faith and degree of fear in the Lord I possess.

God is seeking the righteous man and woman. The perfect person he will never find, and thankfully, that is not the issue. God is looking for one who possesses a heart for him. It has nothing to do with perfection, for the church is glutted with hypocrites, all the way up to the congregational leaders. That is precisely why we so desperately need Jesus and the support of the church, hypocrites and all. We are a fallen people, humanity at large.

God desires commitment from his people. We must decide to commit, or else not. We must choose obedience, or else compromise and sin. We are not following God appropriately if we regard him with most of our lives, and yet, retain certain areas for indulging in sin. A woman may not be eighty percent pregnant. She is either pregnant, or she is not. A person may not follow God eighty percent, and willfully continue in sin the remaining twenty percent. That individual is not following the Lord, and thus, deserting potential blessing. The godly man, in contrast, will continue to falter in areas, but he confesses his sin and returns to God with submissive intent.

Many of us aspire to achieve great things for God, both in this life and for his kingdom to come, to be used by him in some meaningful way. We were created in the image of God for greatness, and to glorify him above all else. I am a firm believer, though, that God will use a person little until the person humbles himself much.

Fact Or Farce

A mental choice must be made as to whether or not the Oracle is indeed real. To believe the prosperity it offers is genuine should logically move an individual to pursue its path with slight compromise. On the other hand, to decide it is a farce, may very well lead a person on a course of immorality with little regard to any consequence that may hypothetically ensue. To choose not to decide or at least remain unemotional to its validity or not, inevitably inclines a person to live a rather dishonorable lifestyle as well. The primary problem, whether one agrees or not, is that man is self-centered and in opposition to God. Paul assures us, "the mind set on the flesh is hostile toward God; for it does not subject itself to the law of God, for it is *not even able* to do so" (Rom. 8:7).

In the mid 1800s, Louis Pasteur was convinced tiny microbes in the air were contaminating food products, including milk, wine, and beer. His ideas sounded absurd. Pasteur expanded his theory that disease stemmed from these minute living microbes, in both animals and humans. The medical field of the day ridiculed his theories. "I am afraid that the experiments you quote, M. Pasteur, will turn against you. The world into which you wish to take us is really too fantastic" (La Presse, 1860).[7] And yet, his discoveries were accurate, ushering in a multitude of vaccinations to combat disease. Today, we still pasteurize milk and other products in recognition of his breakthrough.

The unseen world of microbes seemed too far-fetched to accept the life-altering effects Pasteur claimed. In much the same way, the Oracle may seem too radical to accept. The bold notion of blessing and cursing by an unseen God will undoubtedly be mocked by many skeptics, dismissed by even more with indifference, and embraced by but a few.

THE MONUMENTAL CHOICE

We must select our behaviors wisely. When faced with the opportunity to sin, we will have an important choice to make. Two options will dangle before us, obedience or sin. We either choose faithfulness and pursue the will of God, or rather we follow our own desire. But be cautioned, for life is tailored by the choices we make, and our fate will rest upon the outcome of each test or temptation we encounter.

> How long will you falter between two opinions?
> If the Lord is God, follow Him;
> but if Baal, follow him.
> —1 Kings 18:21

Envision the classic fork in the road scenario, whereupon the traveler must at this moment decide which way to continue his journey. He must select either path A or B, and the outcome of the course to which he commits will prove vastly different than the other route. To paint a more realistic analogy of life, the traveler may not turn back to the way from which he came. He must continue meandering down the unfamiliar path ahead. Nor is he allowed the luxury of determining a path, and upon realizing his error, returning to the fork in order to take the alternate road.

Our decisions map out our life ahead. The choices we make, whether upright or immoral, condition the remainder of our lives. And while forgiveness is readily available for genuine repentance, missed opportunities slip by and consequences still befall. The great news is that God can use the unfavorable outcomes of poor choices for good for the humble soul who seeks him.

Promises of blessing are flooded throughout the Bible. The majority of people neglect to appropriate the benefits for themselves, for most blessings are conditional. This is only one of many reasons to individually dig into the Scriptures, instead of relying solely on the teachings of another. Jump in personally and boldly claim the promises offered, being certain to fulfill the necessary requirements. Voluntarily or not, entire themes and passages of the Bible are overlooked from many a pulpit, or perhaps, if not omitted, loosely misinterpreted.

A random example is found in the first three verses of the book of "The Revelation of Jesus Christ", also known as "The Revelation", or mistakenly called "Revelations". A common misinterpretation of the passage leads many to teach that this is the only book of the Bible that promises a blessing to any who read it. That sounds wonderful and bears a partial truth, but falls shy in accuracy. The verse actually assures a blessing to those who read the book *and heed* the words contained within. A vast difference emanates between heeding and simply reading the words. The blessing arises from obedience to the written word. Many will read, but few will heed.

It matters not if you memorize all of Scripture, if you neither heed nor appropriate the words contained. The value is in the obedience, in the complying and conforming to the wisdom and counsel offered. Possessing the knowledge and promises proves insufficient, for Satan himself comprehends such concepts. No, the truths of God's Word must be *embraced* and *personalized*. The directives must be claimed, internalized, and applied to render benefit to the student.

There are always negative consequences for sin, and a sense of sorrow is left for the transgressor. "Can a man take fire to his bosom, and his clothes not be burned? Can one walk on hot coals, and his feet not be seared?" (Prov. 6:27, 28). The obvious answer to each question is no. If a man voluntarily walks in sin, he will suffer in some fashion. Proverbs warns that "evil pursues sinners, but to the righteous, good shall be repaid" (Prov. 13:21). We are assured, "the eyes of the Lord are in every place, keeping watch on the evil and the good" (Prov. 15:3). How triumphant to the upright and horrid to the perverse as divine blessing and cursing is dispensed accordingly.

Regardless of punishment form, the adversity always outweighs any counterfeit benefit received. Sin is never worth it!

Discover Life

If we are honest and commit time to introspection, we discover we each suffer a void within our soul that may only be filled by God, who skillfully designed us in such fashion. This helps to explain why people groups in every culture worldwide are prone to worship a god of some type. We long to satisfy the barrenness we are unable to fill with belongings, prominence, relationships, and love. Nothing else quenches a thirsty soul in a parched land without God.

The message of the Oracle, the principle of fearing God and honoring him without compromise, is so simple and straightforward. And yet, it remains amazingly profound. It requires meditating upon its precepts to usher revolutionary change within the mind and soul. It demands a paradigm shift in one's thinking, in altering the perspective and directive of one's life. It involves loving God for who he is, without discriminating obedience based upon the gifts he may or may not award. Whether blessed in the present or future, it is knowing the favor of God rests with him. Conversely, though he surrounds himself with possessions, the unfaithful forgo blessing. Wealth remains to that man a temporal and fleeting facade.

Indeed, apart from God, there is nothing on this earth that satisfies the hunger of a longing soul. Each of us must face the monumental decision to pursue God or determine to live a life of isolated independence.

We must desire a new life with a radically different perspective. An individual must be moved toward repentance of his immorality, resulting in a fundamental change in both thought and behavior. Attending a sound church may prove invaluable, but without an altered heart, God is unimpressed. Far too many people embrace a false sense of hope as they attend church each week, and yet they enjoy no real relationship with God. It was Jesus who continually rebuked the hypocritical religious leaders of his day. God is not so much interested with the one or two hours sacrificed on Sunday morning, as he is with all twenty-four hours of every day of your life. If that conjures up images of stress or boredom, a person has completely misunderstood the implications of a life surrendered to God. The person who yields his life to God receives renewed vision. He finds purpose—true purpose. He literally discovers life itself.

Points To Ponder

- We were created in the image of God for greatness, and to glorify him above all else.

- God will use a man little until he humbles himself much.

- Man shall never experience real lasting prosperity until he fears the Lord.

- The message of the Oracle demands a paradigm shift in one's thinking. It involves loving God for who he is, without discriminating obedience based upon the gifts he may or may not award.

- The favor of God rests upon the one who pursues God and his righteousness.

- Apart from God, there is nothing that satisfies or fulfills the hunger of a longing soul.

- Each person must face the monumental decision of either pursuing God, or else determine to live life isolated from him.

- The individual who yields his life to God receives renewed vision and proper perspective, and discovers true purpose.

- Our life is tailored by the choices we make, and our fate will rest upon the outcome of each test or temptation we encounter.

UMBRELLA OF GOD

As many as I love, I rebuke and chasten.
—Revelation 3:19

PARENTAL RESTRAINT

When once we entrust our lives to Christ, we are adopted as children of God. God becomes our rightful and legitimate Father. What a glorious occurrence we so soon take for granted.

Now consider again the analogy between a parent and youth. Children ask for things continuously, some of which are beneficial and others detrimental to the youngster. From love, the parent protects his child by refusing many requests. While an imperfect analogy, God similarly withholds our petitions at times for various reasons.

Paul recites from Isaiah the first commandment with promise: "Honor your father and mother that it may be well with you and you may live long on the earth" (Eph. 6:2, 3). Talk about divine blessing and protection. If we respect and hold our parents in high esteem, it will go well with us and longevity of life may be extended. Just imagine the prosperity potentially forthcoming to those who honor and observe the commands of our *divine* Father!

As our earthly parents discipline us, so our heavenly Father chastens us. The chastening from God may seem harsh at the time, but he does so from love. He aspires to awaken us of our sin and set us upon a proper path. A.W. Tozer offers valuable percep-tiveness suggesting, "it is doubtful whether God can bless a man greatly until He has hurt him deeply".[8] The *hurt* God channels upon his people is meant for good, refinement, and growth.

The aim of the parent should mirror similar goals with his child. In a healthy home, the child retains a wholesome fear of rebellion for repercussions of discipline, and loss of privileges and favor. It is funny how alike the adult compares to the child in the eyes of God. As we desire approval from our heavenly Father, we also need reproof and refinement as we tamper with disobedience.

How sad to observe the child neglected of restraint. His outcome, though perhaps from a loving home, is often comparable to the youth from a home of unloving parents. The proverbs are quite blunt. "He who spares his rod hates his son, but he who loves him disciplines him promptly" (Prov. 13:24). Another adage, "he who hates correction is stupid" (Prov. 12:1), is almost comical with its frankness. Society often frowns upon the discipline of a child, especially that of a mild spanking for reproof. Other avenues of correction are viable, but be slow to judge those who choose to spank. God certainly endorses the option, and a quick reflection upon our turbulent culture today should confirm that something is indeed lacking.

Enough already. Discipline is painful. It is meant to inflict sorrow or loss in order to produce moral behavior. If it were painless, conduct would remain unaltered and we would continue to err to our detriment. Chastisement is profitable and necessary, cultivating the fruit of righteousness to those who take heed of its reproof.

Sodom and Gomorrah demanded severe punishment for their heinous conduct and rebellion toward God. Jonah required a whale of a wake-up call to arouse him from his stubborn resistance to the will of God. Being swallowed by a fish brought necessary compliance and refinement, not to mention a dose of the fear of God. The same occurs today, though the colossal fish consuming us descends behind a different guise altogether.

Power To Transform

Consider the swarm of catastrophes occurring around the globe. Earthquakes, tsunamis, hurricanes, drought, famine, and disease are wreaking havoc more frequently and with greater intensity as time wanes on. The entire world feels the anguish of misery in some way. One may believe these are mere acts of nature and nothing more. But there sits a God behind each of these events, tweaking and manipulating the laws of nature to perform on his behalf.

Then he is an evil and ruthless God, the murmurings rumble. This could not be further from the truth, for God is unbelievably gracious. The fact that any of us breathe today bears witness of his patience and compassion. The devastating events happening around us have transformation of the human soul in mind. They are frequently for reproof, with the aim of drawing the ungodly toward repentance as well as unveiling a fresh perception in the dire need man has for God. The Lord wishes to stir the attention of humanity unto himself and arouse them before it is too late. Still, most of man arrogantly stands and shakes his head at God, for they do not need him. God says they do. Fortunately, in the wake of calamity, a multitude indeed does reevaluate their lives and humbly pursues God.

We must accept trials as either discipline or the manner of God in altering our character for good—or quite possibly, a bit of both. God wishes to transform us to reflect the image of Jesus. This is seldom an easy road. Through times of tribulation and difficult circumstance, God desires for us to build trust, submit to his authority, and learn to lean on him.

But be certain that blessing will cling to the one who fears the Lord. It may not always flesh out according to the manner a person believes it will or should. The faithful steward of God may discover his fate to be a significant loss in earthly standards, possibly the death of a loved one or even himself. This is where trust is tested and refined to the utmost. God will have his best interest for the loyal soul who loves him, and though he himself may breath his last, he dies in the favor of God who holds him dear. He may suddenly be ushered into the presence of God, and all the while, the protective wings of God never parted from around him. God has reasons for outcomes in life, and we must learn to accept and appreciate his unfathomable omniscience. Proverbs 15:16 gently boasts that it is "better to be a poor man in the favor of God than attain great wealth outside His presence."

Shelter Of Prayer

Prayer is unlike any other opportunity we may employ. It remains a unique novelty readily available to us, whereby one may transcend into the dimension and realm of the spiritual world.

If the effective prayer of a righteous man avails much, it goes without saying the prayer of an unrighteous man is deemed ineffective, availing little. The prayers of an ungodly man are spent largely in vain as he persists in dishonoring God with immoral conduct. His prayers prove highly self-centered and fall short of aligning with the will of God. Thus, few answers are realized according to his hopes, and he grows numb to the extraordinary potential prayer offers.

If you lack phone service, it matters not how often or long you speak into the phone. You will not be heard. You must first restore phone service and open the line of communication for each party to effectively converse and be heard. When we live in habitual sin, void of confession and repentance, we are withdrawing communion with God. God will neither associate, nor entertain fellowship with sin. A concept otherwise opposes the very character of sacredness, and contends with the undefiled quality of a hallowed existence.

Renewed fellowship restores divine communication and unfolds the umbrella of God above and around us. As the worries of the world flood down, we may rest beneath the shelter of God, confident he is in sovereign control. What relief when we know he hears in time of need!

WHEN BAD THINGS HAPPEN

Many unfavorable things happen to people for the simple reason of discipline. Genesis tells us a man named Er "was wicked in the sight of the Lord, and the Lord killed him." His brother, Onan, "displeased the Lord; therefore He killed him also" (Gen. 38:7,10).

Sometimes seemingly bad things happen to good people. I say, seemingly, for the hard times in one's life frequently occur for refinement, in order to draw an individual into godly character. We are told, "your iniquities have separated you from your God; and your sins have hidden His face from you, so that He will not hear" (Isa. 59:2). God administers rebuke and purification from a manner of mercy. Looking back, a person may discover the difficult trials were designed for good, though at the time, he blindly stumbled to any such perception.

There are instances when a person may experience suffering and never comprehend why it happened. According to God, Job was a righteous man. He was neither perfect nor sinless, but regarded as blameless for his faith and loyalty to God. And yet, Job suffered monumentally to our standards as he learned of the deaths of his seven children, the loss of his amassed wealth, and his personal acquiring of a horrendous and painful disease. He lost friends, the respect of his community, and his wife encouraged him to curse God and die!

As far as we know, Job never understood why he endured such agony. We are graced the larger picture as God relays the discourse in heaven, where Satan accuses Job of living righteously for the mere sake of God's goodness. Remove the blessings, and Job will turn from God. We have the benefit of understanding that while God allowed Satan to do so, it was Satan who actually caused the devastation. We may also glean the wisdom in trusting God no matter what befalls. God works in ways unfathomable to man and he owes no explanation for the manner in which he moves. God desires that we trust him, regardless of present situation, and wants us to realize he is worthy of our reliance, even amidst suffering.

Solomon instructs a man to pursue God and his righteousness, *regardless* of potential consequence, for choosing otherwise will wrong his soul. God is pleased when we submit to his authority even when we fail to comprehend his reasoning. As we learn to trust more abundantly, our maturity develops more fully. When we entrust the whole of our being to God, including life, finances, family, and personal health, God smiles and his favor rests upon us. *That is a successful life to God!*

THE FAVOR OF GOD

There is little more comforting than the peace that comes from basking in the favor of God. Not only is God on the person's side, but he is *actively* working on his behalf. A word of caution is due here, however, as many a pastor leads his congregation into believing the favor of God is upon them *all*. The subtle slant of truth is generally overlooked, and yet the peace and protection it affords to so many is damnably false.

Does God wish his favor toward all *mankind*? Yes, he wishes that none should perish, and yet most of the world willfully rejects him. Does God desire his favor upon all *believers*? Of course, though an "ungodly" number of believers endure in their sin, with little respect for the fear of the Lord. They neither fear God, nor the consequence of their behavior. So while they may reserve a place in the household of God, their rebellion holds them in a state of corrective consequence, with intention of luring them back toward the God they "love". The favor of God was with the Israelites throughout the Old Testament, as they were his chosen people, and at the same time, they consistently wallowed in dire straits as result of their wickedness.

It reminds me of a similar mistaken belief backed by many that God hears all prayers. As we touched on this before, it sounds nice and flowery, and he is certainly capable of effortlessly hearing millions of prayers simultaneously. The problem is that Scripture teaches otherwise. The prayers of an unrepentant unbeliever are *not* heard. Thankfully, those of a repentant soul are graciously noticed. A person must continually look to the source of God's words for veracity, while wading through fluffy pulpit messages designed to appease a spiritually starved crowd while simultaneously offending none.

God Is For You

Akin to the favor of God, everyone has undoubtedly heard at some point that God is for you. Worry not, for he is on your side. Let us ponder this a moment. Is the Lord, in fact, on your side? Most churches teach a definitive *yes*, across the board to their congregations. It sounds good, feels warm and safe, and the message is comforting to its listeners. Unfortunately, it is only partially true, and the cotton candy clouds render a disservice to a wealth of church-goers.

We encourage far too many politically correct preachers offering flowery, motivational speeches to their congregations. We part the braver church who offends by speaking a bolder truth. Many churches cowardly fortify their numbers by watering down or simply disregarding self-discriminating parts of Scripture in order to safeguard upsetting its members. The world needs fewer politically correct pastors willing to insult for the sake of painting both the love *and* righteous fury of a holy God. We need more godly preachers unwilling to compromise the clear principles of the Word of God for the sake of potentially jeopardizing their personal paycheck.

Jesus died for all sinners, for everyone in the world. I have a difficult time, though, believing God is on the side of those actively rejecting his offer of salvation, or even those completely indifferent to its message. God still wishes them to repent and turn to him, but he may well be working against them presently toward this pursuit. The umbrella of God, so to speak, has yet to fabricate above them as they choose to live independently of him.

Now for the believer, God is for you ultimately, no question. He is a guide, guard, deliverer, and rewarder to those who love him. David tells us the "angel of the Lord encamps all around those who fear Him, and delivers them." What could possibly harm the person completely surrounded by God? David urges us to "fear the Lord, you His saints! There is no want to those who fear Him...those who seek the Lord shall not lack any good thing" (Ps. 34:7, 9, 10). What powerful and encouraging words!

A problem arises, however, for the believer living a lifestyle of intentional sin. He embraces a pattern of willful immorality, and instead of turning from sin, he runs toward it. God cannot tolerate this type of lifestyle, and must dispense discipline in hopes of drawing the wanderer back toward a life of godliness. When we choose to live contrary to the rules of God, we invite his inevitable judgment instead of blessing.

Is God still for this prodigal son of his? Does he remain on his side? Without a doubt, God is still for this soul! But he may very well be aggressively working presently *against* this man or woman for his or her ultimate good. God treats the believer as his son or daughter, and corrects him or her so. God administers trials, correction, confusion, adversity, afflictions, and misfortune to the one in rebellion. If a person discovers he is eluding discipline, be warned, for he may consider himself a child of God, when in fact, he is not. He is an illegitimate child instead (Heb. 12:7-9).

So is God on your side? Well, yes and no, depending upon the individual and his submission to the authority of God. The same applies to a country at large. I submit, if a nation would simply return to God, the gates of hell could do nothing to deter the blessings God would bestow upon that land.

Points To Ponder

- The chastening from God may seem harsh at the time, but he does so out of love. He aspires to awaken us of our sin and set us upon a more noble and proper path, a path of righteousness and obedience.

- Discipline is painful, and meant to inflict sorrow or loss in order to produce morally and godly behavior.

- We must accept trials as either discipline or the manner of God in altering our character for good.

- God has reasons for outcomes in life, and we must learn to accept and appreciate his unfathomable omniscience.

- God desires that we trust him, regardless of our present situation. God wants us to realize that he is worthy of our trust, even amidst suffering.

- When a man entrusts the whole of his life to God, God smiles, and his favor rests upon him. *That is a successful life to God!*

- When we choose to live contrary to the ways and rules of God, we invite his inevitable judgment instead of blessing.

- God often administers trials, correction, confusion, adversity, afflictions, and misfortune to the one in rebellion to his ways.

God Loves Sacrifice

Whoever offers praise glorifies Me;
and to him who orders his conduct aright
I will show the salvation of God.
—Psalm 50:23

God loves sacrifice. Think about that for a moment. An infinite Being delights in the sacrifices offered by his creation. What does it mean to sacrifice? Simply put, to sacrifice is to give up something you would rather hold onto. The God of the universe receives pleasure when man surrenders something he would rather maintain. A self-sufficient God needs nothing, and yet, he delights when man yields something of personal value over to him. How can this relinquishing be cherished by such a boundless God?

Sacrifice is such an expression of the spirit, it rightfully constitutes a fundamental part of worship. God wants a person to outwardly express the genuine state of his will, demonstrate where his true allegiance lies, and display his faithfulness to the God he loves. God is actively watching the believer to see if he complies with the sacrifices he requires. God is seeking to bless the man who owns a loyal and rightful attitude toward him and the manner of living to which he calls.

Sacrifice Of Righteousness

Men love the darkness, and befittingly so, for wicked deeds and thoughts are best performed in secret. But the lure of sin is a

155

facade. The enticements of greed and selfishness are destructive attributes of self-centeredness in the pursuit of attaining more and more for the betterment of oneself. Cheating on taxes and fraudulent business practices are thefts and close cousins to greed in the quest for unlawful gain. While the improper action may seem to escape notice, in reality it never does. God sees all, and consequences befall the offender, regardless of whether the transgressor associates the penalizing effects with the root cause or not. The cause and effect relationship is reliable and real.

Some sins are sensually or mentally pleasurable. Sexual fornication runs rampant to fulfill the temporary temptations of inappropriate fleshly desires. Gluttony is a short-lived gratification of an ever-growing condition that refuses to diminish. Even passing judgment upon others increases our sense of pride and self-importance as we indulge upon their inferior spiritual, mental, or physical character.

The root of immorality is allegiance to *self*, as one inaudibly, yet distinctly, avows *my will* instead of *thy will* be done. How can I better serve *myself*? What is beneficial to *me*?

While God calls us to a life of righteousness, he recognizes the appropriate choice is a sacrifice. Sin often comes easily and with pleasurable carnal benefit—a deceptive benefit bearing root to ill effects. To choose a lifestyle honoring God, even in privacy and beyond the public eye, is a yielding of our self. Turning from immorality toward morality is a conscious choice, placing God above our own desires and ambitions. The righteousness exacted by God requires a clearly defined paradigm shift in the mind of the faithful individual.

While upright behavior is a sacrifice, how ironic what we deny ourselves is merely conduct characterized by perversity, depravity, destruction, and personal detriment. "But know that the Lord has set apart for Himself him who is godly; the Lord will hear when I call to Him … offer the sacrifices of righteousness, and put your trust in the Lord" (Ps. 4:3,5). A life pursuit of God is a surrender of will, purpose, and design, that in reality brings true freedom and unimaginable blessing.

SACRIFICE OF THANKSGIVING

Complaining comes easily for most of us. Far from satisfying or pleasing, for some odd reason, it feels gratifying to release a murmur now and then regarding imperfect conditions. God takes our grumbling surprisingly serious, for an ungrateful attitude parallels the state of our heart and the depth of our trust. Throughout the Old Testament, the Israelites expressed their pessimism and bitterness again and again. God is merciful, but even they produced a holy fury from the Lord with their repetitive complaining.

God is looking for an attitude of persistent praise, even when things go awry. A thankful spirit, regardless of circumstance, bears testimony that God is in control. He makes no mistakes and nothing slips by his care without his allowance. Remaining thankful also evidences our trust, as we affirm that "all things work together for good to those who love God, to those who are the called according to His purpose" (Rom. 8:28). Seemingly bad things do happen with those he loves, and yet, they occur for good and pure reasons. Unfavorable outcomes may serve to strengthen our walk with God, deepen our faith, or prune our lives of immorality.

A spirit of discontentment begins subtly, slowly developing into an unsuspecting habit, and morphing into a plague before the host is ever aware. The personal affliction is extremely infectious, and must be treated as such, or those nearby will fall victim to its virus. We must quarrel with this spirit of ungratefulness, and mentally pursue a worshipful heart.

We are called by God to be joyful, to actively *choose* joy. It may not always prove easy or effortless, and he recognizes this reality. But how encouraging that an attitude of joy and thankfulness is similarly highly contagious!

God knows all will not turn out as we wish, and so it is indeed a sacrifice to offer praise no matter what occurs. "Let them sacrifice the sacrifices of thanksgiving, and declare His works with rejoicing" (Ps. 107:22). The author of Hebrews invites us to "continually offer the sacrifice of praise to God, that is, the fruit of our lips, giving thanks to His name. But do not forget to do good and to share, for with such sacrifices God is well pleased" (Heb. 13:15, 16).

How inspiring to know when we surrender something of value for the sake of God, he is not only pleased, but *well* pleased. What an honor to literally move God with joy and summon a smile upon his face. What could possibly be more rewarding than that?

Acknowledge the real source of lasting joy, and determine to seize optimism and offer praise. Find a reason to give thanks each day, regardless of present conditions, for the joy of the Lord is your strength!

Sacrifice Of Resources

The apostle Paul tells us, "God loves a cheerful giver" (2 Cor. 9:7). We readily associate giving with money, but also pleasing to God are other resources as we surrender them over to his stewardship. We might offer time, talent, and wisdom to fulfill the needs of another. God understands our personal possessions and abilities are limited, and he is well pleased when we release them for his purposes.

So just how much are we obliged to give? At what point is God satisfied with our contributions that we might then receive his blessing? If these are questions stirring within us, we have yet to comprehend the intent of giving God is seeking. I imagine a sliding scale of selfless giving I call *dimensional giving.*

I liken first dimensional giving with a child who learns to share with his sibling. He comes to understand that not only will the toy he shares return to him, but he will get to play with the toys of his sibling, a win-win situation.

Second dimensional giving is like assisting a family member or good friend. You may not receive anything in return, but at least it has been invested within the family or friendship, and they love you for it.

Third dimensional giving occurs when a person gives to another, be it possessions, time, or a meal, but in his heart he expects to be reimbursed at some point. In his mind he is "ahead by one", and while he gave out of love, the individual he helped is now implicitly indebted to him.

Finally, fourth dimensional giving takes place when you give and recognize you will not receive back, at least not in the ordinary sense of repayment. This might include donating to orphanages, missions, evangelical outreaches, and those suffering hunger or sickness.

The caution here, for there exists an ever-present danger shadowing any good or pure action, is to render without self-righteous motives. We all love a pat on the back, even if others merely realize the significance of our offering. Fourth dimensional giving runs almost parallel with the spiritual dimension, where God alone is the one who rewards. I challenge you to give something anonymously without anyone knowing you gave it, only you and God as witness.

God is observing the intent of your heart. Will you bless others as God has blessed you? He desires from us a quality of heart, for us to recognize that everything we have and all we are is truly from God. And while a specific measure of sacrifice is not necessarily the issue, the danger remains of erring on the side of robbing God with appropriating too little.

SACRIFICE BY FASTING

A friend once informed me he was giving up cursing for a month to satisfy his religious duty at the time. That seemed a silly objective to me for his choice of fast. While I can appreciate and respect the challenge of speaking more wholesomely, if the aim is simply temporary, perhaps it signals a perverted purpose. The goal suggests more of a fulfillment of religion, and less an intimate relationship with the proper object of said religion. If the desire to cease cursing is genuine, that is more appropriately termed repentance, as one seeks to turn from a shameful manner of behavior in order to better walk in the likeness of Christ.

Fasting generally involves surrendering something for a time, and then welcoming it back upon the timely completion of the fast. While a fast may constitute a need, want, or particular habit, it most often comprises food. The thing fasted upon is rarely considered a bad thing in itself, but likely something wholesome. Again, abandoning a sin is wonderful and essential, but that is not a fast. That is a given, and the poor behavior should not be revisited.

Jesus told his followers that when they fast, instead of making an outward show of it, they should not appear to be fasting. The Father "who is in the secret place," he explained, "sees in secret" and "will reward you openly" (Matt. 6:16—18). Interestingly, Jesus said *when* you fast, as opposed to *if* you fast, as fasting represented a common practice. Jesus later informed the disciples that certain prayers are only answered through prayer and fasting.

Fasting physically has a way of arousing a greater awareness and sensitivity spiritually. It should be accompanied with the confession of one's sins, and may prove beneficial in seeking God's will and direction, petitioning help, and kindling a deeper intimacy with God.

As God is concerned with both the physical and spiritual needs of his people, it is sometimes profitable to forfeit a bodily desire or necessity for the sake of benefiting the spiritual.

SACRIFICE OF SELF

A person may utter, "I love you," a million times to a loved one, but it may resonate superficially until he affirms through action. There are countless ways to communicate love, but nothing demonstrates it as intimately as sacrifice. When one surrenders something of value for the sake of someone else, it sends a profound message.

The Oracle calls us to fear the Lord by loving God wholeheartedly. Since love is manifested most notably through sacrifice, we are to render our entire being to the one who gave us life. God loves, most of all, the sacrifice of a broken spirit, for until the spirit of man is humbled and pride surrendered, he continues to rely on his own merits.

Jesus offered the ultimate sacrifice. Because he was sinless, his death was sufficient to serve as punishment on behalf of the sinner, fully assuming the wrath of God toward sin. How absurd for deity to suffer an inhumane and unwarranted death on account of his own creation! And yet, he did precisely that. How altogether wonderful his mercy toward mankind. It should move us with joy to render our lives for the advancement of his will and glory.

Unfortunately, sometimes a sacrifice is offered from mere habit or custom, with little meaning behind the action. We must remember that simple obedience to God is always more appropriate than any sacrifice we muster. Solomon confirms that performing "righteousness and justice is more acceptable to the Lord than sacrifice" (Prov. 21:3). Likewise, the prophet Samuel tells us God receives more pleasure when we obey him rather than when we offer ritualistic sacrifice (1 Sam. 15:22). Heart intent *always* trumps physical ritual or tradition.

Points To Ponder

- Sacrifice is such an expression of the spirit, it rightfully constitutes a fundamental part of worship.

- The root of immorality is allegiance to self, as one inaudibly, yet distinctly, avows *my will* instead of *thy will* be done.

- The righteousness exacted by God requires a clearly defined paradigm shift in the mind.

- A life pursuit of God and holiness is a surrender of will, purpose, and design, that in reality, brings true freedom and unimaginable blessing.

- God takes our grumbling surprisingly serious, for an ungrateful attitude parallels the state of our heart and the depth of our trust in him.

- God understands our personal possessions and abilities are limited, and he is well pleased when we release them for his purposes.

- While a specific measure of sacrifice is not necessarily the issue, the danger remains of erring on the side of robbing God with giving too little.

- There are countless ways to communicate love, but nothing demonstrates it as well as sacrifice.

- Simple obedience to God is always more appropriate than any sacrifice we muster.

WHO CLAIMED THE ORACLE?

Whether it is pleasing or displeasing,
we will obey the voice of the Lord our God ...
that it may be well with us when we obey the voice
of the Lord our God.
—Jeremiah 42:6

What an inspiring verse! Oh, that we would each arrive at the uncommon, yet extraordinary abode of unbridled commitment to God. Even when it means doing the unfavorable, we may remain confident the end result will indeed prove favorable as we follow God.

God pours his favor upon those who follow the Oracle, to the faithful few committed to obedience. A number of these loyal followers are expanded upon in the Bible and serve inspirational testimonies of a loving God who yearns to bless his people as they pursue him diligently. The following are but a few who experienced firsthand the radical principle and ensuing prosperity of the Oracle.

DANIEL

When Jerusalem was besieged by Babylon, King Nebuchadnezzar ordered the best-looking and gifted Israelites to be taken to serve before the king. Daniel, along with three of his friends, Hananiah, Mishael, and Azariah, were chosen for the honor to serve. For their faithfulness, God blessed these men with knowledge, skill, and wisdom, far beyond those who already served the king.

God moved on behalf of these men, and Daniel was soon promoted to ruler of the entire province of Babylon and over all its wise men. Likewise, his friends were assigned as managers over the affairs of Babylon. From a defeated Jerusalem, it was no small feat for these Israelites to lead a foreign nation. But the Bible tells us God appoints rulers and sways the king where he wills.

Years later, King Darius assumed kingship of Babylon. He signed a decree mandating if anyone petitioned a god or man for thirty days besides the king, he was to be cast into the lions den. Daniel feared God, and only God, and as was his custom, he continued praying in his home several times each day. Once discovered, the king was regrettably forced to throw Daniel into the den of lions. God sent an angel to shut the mouths of the lions, and Daniel was spared. Not only did Daniel prosper, we are told, but King Darius issued a new decree stating that all men within his entire kingdom must tremble and fear the God of Daniel. Talk about an instant shift in the allegiance and worship of a king and nation!

Hananiah, Mishael, and Azariah

Perhaps better known by their Babylonian names, Shadrach, Meshach, and Abed-Nego fared a similar fate as Daniel. When King Nebuchadnezzar constructed a ninety foot statue of gold, he ordered all peoples and nations to fall down and worship whenever they heard the sounding of specified instruments. Shadrach, Meshach, and Abed-Nego refused to worship any god or image other than the one true God. This went over horribly, as one might imagine, and they were cast into a fiery furnace heated seven times hotter than normal. Though the men who pushed them into the furnace were killed from intense heat, the three Jewish friends were unharmed. Once the king observed not only the three of them walking around in the furnace, but also a fourth, with the form "like the Son of God", he called them to return from the fire.

With no harm upon the men, nor even the smell of smoke, the king blessed their God and issued a new decree. Anyone who merely spoke against the God of Shadrach, Meshach, and Abed-Nego would be sliced into pieces, for there exists no other God able to save as this. The king then promoted, or literally "caused to prosper," the three men. Honor God, and he will honor you.

SOLOMON

When Solomon became king of Israel, he loved the Lord. One evening, God appeared to Solomon in a dream. "What shall I give you?" God inquired. "Just ask!" As a young king around twenty years of age, Solomon asked for understanding and discernment between good and evil, that he might effectively rule and judge his people. God was pleased with the heart of Solomon, and he blessed him with more wisdom and understanding than any before or after him.

The Lord is a generous God, and since Solomon had neither sought wealth nor honor, God gave these, too, in abundance. Because he chose to glorify God with his life, God set Solomon apart, and gladly exalted him above and beyond all other kings. The dream ended with an additional, conditional promise. If Solomon continued to fear God and obey his commandments, he would prolong his life on top of it all!

JOB

"There was a man in the land of Uz, whose name was Job; and that man was blameless and upright, and one who feared God and shunned evil" (Job 1:1). Job *feared* God. He shunned evil, literally meaning he *turned* from evil. Job lived in prosperity.

The attributes of Satan may be painted with an unusually

diverse palette. Satan is arrogant, deceptive, rebellious, dishonest, and self-centered. He is unwise and will ultimately end in failure. He is a fool, for *anyone* attempting to exalt himself above God would be regarded as such. Satan is undoubtedly beautiful, unlike the silly modern depiction of a crimson body with horns, tail, and pitchfork. He is certainly clever, insightful, and perceptive.

If Satan comprehends one thing, it is the principle of the Oracle. He understands if a soul fears the Lord, God blesses him with protection, life, and prosperity. Lucifer, at one time, possessed these blessings himself. But forfeiting his position and status, he presently seeks to lure as many from God as possible. "Does Job fear God for nothing?" Satan asked God. "Have You not made a hedge around him … You have blessed the work of his hands, and his possessions have increased in the land" (Job 1:9, 10).

As previously mentioned, Satan recognized the correlation between fearing God and prosperity. Obey God and acquire blessing. Disobey God and be cursed. Satan believed the only reason Job feared the Lord was to inherit the good fortune that followed. Withhold the blessing, adding adversity instead, and Job would abandon his integrity and reject God. His fear of the Lord hinged on whether or not he flourished. We know God allowed Satan to test his challenge, and amidst devastation, Job remained faithful. After a time of testing, Job again was blessed for turning from evil and fearing God.

Noah

God looked upon the world, and every intent of man was corrupt. God said he was sorry for having made man, and finally decided to destroy the human race.

But wait. One man walked with God. Perfect? Of course not, but a man who feared the Lord. God found *one* man. One obedient soul would prove worthy and sufficient to alter the course of human history from that day forward. God would spare this solitary man, and with his family, prosper him and begin the world anew.

Hebrews tells us, "by faith Noah, being divinely warned of things not yet seen, moved with *godly fear*, prepared an ark for the saving of his household (Heb. 11:7, italics added). God blessed his family and renewed in them the mission to be fruitful and multiply upon the earth. Oh, what height of splendor God is willing to accomplish through the *individual* who holds him in high esteem!

ABRAHAM

God promised Abraham his descendants would be numerous, like the stars in the sky. God declared that Abraham's wife would soon be blessed with a son. Sarah was already ninety years old, a bit of a challenge in the reasoning of the elderly couple, yet to God, mere child's play. To their joy and amazement, Sarah conceived and gave birth to Isaac. God oftentimes works in ways that seem unreasonable or impossible to man, which only attests to his grandeur and omnipotence.

When Isaac was a young boy, God decided to test the heart of Abraham. Would he love God or his son, Isaac, more? He was ordered to offer his son as a burnt offering in the land of Moriah, about a three day journey away. This seemed not only harsh, but illogical, for God promised that the son of Abraham would boast a multitude of descendants. Now God wanted Abraham to kill Isaac! Whether Abraham believed God would provide a replacement for the offering, or else he would raise Isaac from the dead, he did not delay in complying. After likely the worst night of his life, he rose early the following morning to embark on the ominous trip.

When they arrived, Abraham built an altar and placed his bound son atop it. He clutched the knife that was to take the life of his son, and Abraham heard an audible voice from God. "Do not lay your hand on the lad, or do anything to him; for I know that you fear God, since you have not withheld your son, your only son, from Me" (Gen. 22:12). It was only a test. Abraham proved he feared the Lord, no matter the cost. As a result of Abraham's obedience, God promised he would bless him and his descendants.

JOSEPH

At the age of seventeen, the eleven jealous brothers of Joseph sold him into slavery to Midianite traders. They reported to their father he had surely been killed by a wild beast. The Midianites, meanwhile, journeyed to Egypt, where they sold Joseph to a high-ranking officer of Pharaoh. What an awful week for Joseph, abandoned by his brothers and sold as a slave in a foreign land. Where was God? Why does he allow such unspeakable things to happen, especially to someone who loves the Lord? It seems both unreasonable and unfair. And yet, God is able to use negative conditions for good.

Joseph became a slave, but we are told the Lord was with him, and caused him to prosper. His master perceived Joseph possessed the favor of God, and that "the Lord made all he did to prosper in his hand" (Gen. 39:3). He was later falsely accused of a wrong and sent to prison. And yet, we are told again "the Lord was with him; and whatever he did, the Lord made it prosper" (Gen. 39:23).

By the time he was thirty, Joseph was governor over all Egypt, with only Pharaoh ruling above him! God used Joseph to spare countless people, including his own brothers and family, from impending famine throughout the land. What man meant for harm, God intended for good.

THE ORDINARY MAN

These are but a taste of testimonies of those who honored God and enjoyed prosperity. Each of these individuals, and countless others, accomplished extraordinary things in their lifetime. We would do well to remember, though, that like you and me, these were simply ordinary men and women, except for one thing. One thing set them apart from others. *They feared the Lord.*

God wants to bless today, as he did the man and woman through whom he first breathed life. Blessing was grossly forfeited as sin entered the world, but with repentance, restoration with God, and renewed purpose, hope abounds. Present and future blessing is still promised, but the terms are conditional. Prosperity lies well within the reach of every soul who truly, but truly, fears the Lord.

Points To Ponder

- When following God means doing something unfavorable, we may remain confident the end result will prove favorable.

- God appoints rulers and sways man where he wills.

- The person who fears God will invariably shun and turn from evil.

- Even Satan comprehends the Oracle, and the correlation between fearing God and dwelling in prosperity.

- God is willing to accomplish unfathomable things through the *individual* who honors him.

- God often moves in seemingly unreasonable and impossible ways.

- Sometimes God uses difficult circumstances for good purpose, and in a manner that brings glory to God.

- To move mountains, one thing sets apart the ordinary man and woman from all others. They fear God.

- Prosperity lies well within the reach of each soul who truly fears the Lord. Hope abounds with repentance, restoration with God, and renewed purpose.

CONCLUSION

Let us hear the conclusion of the whole matter:
Fear God and keep His commandments, for this is man's all.
For God will bring every work into judgment,
including every secret thing, whether good or evil.
—Ecclesiastes 12:13, 14

A HIGHER CALLING

The verse just prior to the ones penned above is notable as the author wisely asserts, "of making many books there is no end, and much study is wearisome to the flesh." But this is the conclusion, he continues, the grand finale. If *anything* is learned, he instructs, know *this*! The entire duty of man, his highest responsibility, his personal reason for being is to *fear the Lord God and heed his commands*. The Oracle cuts straight to the heart of our existence!

Matthew urges us to "seek first the kingdom of God and His righteousness, and all these things shall be added to you" (Matt. 6:33). Moses assures us, "the Lord will prosper you ... the Lord will again rejoice over you for good ... *if you turn to the Lord your God with all your heart and with all your soul*" (Deut. 30:5, 9, 10). The italics were added for emphasis, for they are key. There must be a turning, a change of mind, from a self-absorbed life to one centered upon God. God knows whether we truly desire him, or simply the benefits he may provide.

On the other hand, an individual may choose to go it alone, and forfeit the blessing of God and fulfillment in life he offers. Every outcome in life will be conditioned by the paramount decision of either clinging to God or else rejecting him. A radical shift in one's reasoning is critical, from a self-serving mentality to one of humble obedience. Self must be removed from the throne of one's life and God ushered into its place. For an individual to discover purpose and meaning in life, he must desperately pursue the Oracle.

Knowing the favor of God rests upon us as we choose to fear him, a question begs each of us. Am I seeking God and conforming my life to his standards in order to gain prosperity? While this line of reasoning is not entirely frowned upon, as God himself challenges us with ensuing reward, hopefully a deeper motivation impassionates us in following him.

Fear the Lord and discover a blessed life with the favor of God. Do not take my word for it, though. We have but lightly brushed a few of the innumerable verses exhorting us to fear God and walk in his ways. Fulfillment, purpose, and prosperity are promised only to the one who responds and commits to this higher calling in life.

The Profound Choice

As already established, a decision must be made, and in all likelihood, a daily occurrence it will be. Either we honor God and fulfill his will, or else we disobey by preferring an alternate path. Choices in varying degrees will continually surface, bearing enticing options, some good and others not so good. Will a subtle compromise lure us astray? It is often the small choices that prove paramount in our walk with God. If we dislike someone, it remains elementary in refraining from murdering that individual. An easy choice it is to make, so the reward in refraining is quite miniscule. On the other hand, choosing not to gossip or resisting the temptation to flirt with immorality will generally prove more challenging.

God is actively observing the minor choices we make daily, which in actuality, are critical decisions in our pursuit toward godliness and an intimate relationship with God. Never under-estimate how crucial each compromise we face bears witness in conditioning the remainder of our lives. Walking in obedience also yields an inexplicable ability to render God delight and plea-sure. What a remarkable opportunity we possess!

EXAMINE THE MESSAGE SOURCE

Prosperity messages and get-rich-quick schemes dangle before us relentlessly. Most prey upon the naive. The prosperity peddler lurks on the television in the dead of night for the desperate indi-vidual, offering to send a therapeutic prayer cloth, if only he sends a financial gift of faith. He divinely observes a man with chronic back pain who will receive healing with a gift of one hundred dollars or more. He imagines the hundreds of people sleeplessly lying awake in pain as they watch him articulate with empathy for their welfare. He almost appears to care for them!

Another disguises his lectures of good fortune as sermons, week after week, preying upon thousands of gullible souls long-ing for an easier, more comfortable lifestyle. He presents a slickly groomed message in his shiny, expensive suit, of God giving everyone everything they want. The pews fill effortlessly, as he spoon feeds his hungry sheep. Beaming a cocky smile from ear to ear, he exposes magnificently white teeth, and argues how we all deserve to be wealthy. "You deserve that grand job, that distinguished house you have always dreamed of," he hypes en-thusiastically. Why, he owns the lofty mansion himself to prove it! Curious, how God affirms otherwise.

"You just have to believe," continues the preacher warmly. The mega church attendees lean closer and eagerly listen to his persistent peddling. "God is for you; he is working on your behalf. Just reach out in faith and believe it. Go ahead. Ask for that nice car! Pray for that ideal parking spot as you pull into the mall. You will get it!" he ensures with a sparkle in his eye.

These are lies and the pastor a deceiver. He voices a partial truth, only the part, of course, that sounds pleasant and gratifying. He intentionally fails to mention God is actually working *against* the person who turns his back on him and lives in sin. Woe to that man who dupes his flock and leads them astray!

Still another insists her readers of the innate power we may harness to instruct the universe to move on our behalf. With the universal law of attraction, she targets the trusting persons pursuing a simple solution to fulfilling their every whim. Like waving a magic wand, one may wish whatever they want, and if he believes hard enough, the universe has no choice but to compensate him with his lust. He is a magnet dictating all he desires, for he is all powerful. He is his own god. Alas, he *is* god! He is also deceived, for the only one receiving benefit is the inventor of such a silly notion. But that's her little secret.

It is crucial to examine the source of the message. These pitches may very well include some glimmer of truth. But these speak for either selfish gain or suffer delusion themselves. Certainly, God can provide the perfect parking space, for nothing is impossible to him. Believing we can accomplish something may help one excel by inspiring necessary confidence for completing a successful task. But be cautious, for partial truths are generally the deadliest. They are subtle distortions that fabricate and mislead the one seeking a pure truth.

Satan himself quoted verses from God's Word to support his claims, yet he invariably twisted the intent for selfish motive. Always check the source and context with the Word of God. If it cannot be backed up in the Scriptures, and for certain if it stands contrary to them, be suspect. Never walk in blind faith. It is imperative to validate what is spoken with an authoritative source.

EVALUATE YOUR INTENT

There are few guarantees in this life. Even the principles established by God are general universal laws. Many promises of God are conditional, based on behavior and obedience to His Word. To those who follow and love him, God promises prosperity, including peace incomprehensible apart from him. The man searching riches as his number one priority may be appalled when he does not acquire them. If after earnestly pursuing God, we grow enraged for lack of wealth, we are undoubtedly missing an integral part of seeking God wholeheartedly. Our chief aim is indeed *us* with this response, and we would be wise to reevaluate our passion and intent. In the end, we must each learn to trust God completely, regardless of circumstance. We must thrive to maturity and increase in faith, entrusting to him fully our wills, desires, lives, and fates.

The deeper our love for God develops, the easier it becomes to follow without wandering, for love and obedience go hand in hand relentlessly, as two sides of the same coin. We must never forget with love comes sacrifice. Raising children is a sacrifice, but our love for them makes it all worthwhile. Enjoying a rich and happy marriage involves continual sacrifice on the part of each spouse. Unfortunately, innumerable marriages fall apart as we refuse to yield our self-serving desires for the other. Forsaking sinful desires is indeed a sacrifice.

The goal in life is not to receive blessing and prosperity as its ultimate end. The focus must be taken off ourselves and centered upon God. *Our purpose, rather, is to fear God by glorifying and honoring him through godly living.* That is the *pathway to prosperity*, the blessings of which are merely the merciful icing upon the cake of life.

POINTS TO PONDER

- There must be a turning, a change of mind, from a self-absorbed life to one centered upon God.

- Self must be removed from the throne of an individual's life, and God ushered into its place.

- Fulfillment, purpose, and prosperity are promised only to the one who responds and commits to the higher calling of the Oracle.

- It is oftentimes the small choices we make that prove paramount in our walk with God.

- Never underestimate how crucial each compromise we face bears witness in conditioning the remainder of our lives.

- Walking in obedience yields an inexplicable ability to render Almighty God both delight and pleasure.

- Partial truths are generally the deadliest, representing subtle distortions that mislead the one seeking a pure truth.

- Remember, the aim in life is not to receive blessing and prosperity as its ultimate goal. Focus must be removed from ourselves. Our purpose is to fear God by glorifying and honoring Him through godly living.

Closing Challenge

Behold, the eye of the Lord is
on those who fear Him.
—Psalm 33:18

Meditate

Read and meditate upon the following verses, as God instructs
the Israelites on experiencing a blessed life. Thousands of years
later, the message and means to prosperity remains precisely the
same. The Word of God is just as true, alive, and active today for
any who will turn to God.

Deuteronomy 28:1—20, 29

"Now it shall come to pass, *if* you diligently obey the voice of
the Lord your God, to observe carefully all His commandments
which I command you today, that the Lord your God will set you
high above all nations of the earth. And all these blessings shall
come upon you and overtake you, *because* you obey the voice of
the Lord your God:

Blessed shall you be in the city, and blessed shall you be in
the country.

Blessed shall be the fruit of your body, the produce of your
ground and the increase of your herds, the increase of your cattle
and the offspring of your flocks.

Blessed shall be your basket and your kneading bowl.

Blessed shall you be when you come in, and blessed shall you be when you go out.

The Lord will cause your enemies who rise against you to be defeated before your face; they shall come out against you one way, and flee before you seven ways.

The Lord will command the blessing on you in your storehouses and in all to which you set your hand, and He will bless you in the land which the Lord your God is giving you.

The Lord will establish you as a holy people to Himself, just as He has sworn to you, *if* you keep the commandments of the Lord your God and walk in His ways. Then all peoples of the earth shall see that you are called by the name of the Lord, and they shall be afraid of you. And the Lord will grant you plenty of goods, in the fruit of your body, in the increase of your livestock, and in the produce of your ground, in the land of which the Lord swore to your fathers to give you. The Lord will open to you His good treasure, the heavens, to give the rain to your land in its season, and to bless all the work of your hand. You shall lend to many nations, but you shall not borrow. And the Lord will make you the head and not the tail; you shall be above only, and not be beneath, *if* you heed the commandments of the Lord your God, which I command you today, and are careful to observe them. So you shall not turn aside from any of the words which I command you this day, to the right or the left, to go after other gods to serve them.

But it shall come to pass, if you do not obey the voice of the Lord your God, to observe carefully all His commandments and His statutes which I command you today, that all these curses will come upon you and overtake you:

Cursed shall you be in the city, and cursed shall you be in the country.

Cursed shall be your basket and your kneading bowl.

Cursed shall be the fruit of your body and the produce of your land, the increase of your cattle and the offspring of your flocks.

Cursed shall you be when you come in, and cursed shall you be when you go out.

The Lord will send on you cursing, confusion, and rebuke in all that you set your hand to do...you shall not prosper in your ways; you shall be only oppressed and plundered continually, and no one shall save you."

You Must Act

You may conclude these passages apply exclusively to the Israelites thousands of years ago. Huge mistake! As surely as the Israelites were the chosen people of God, so too, are present believers. The blessings and curses are as binding and applicable to those who presently trust in God. But the promises are conditional, so in order to reap the benefits, you must act.

The Oracle is offered to anyone who will listen and heed its message. You may remain indifferent toward it, you may dismiss it, or you may embrace it. Those are the options, and only those who adopt its precepts will discover true prosperity. But it refuses to shout. The Oracle whispers to you now. What will *you* do with the Oracle?

The world has all but lost the fear of the Lord. God is scouring the Earth to find the one who will take his holiness seriously and honor his Word through obedience. It is impossible to run toward both God and sin simultaneously. You must choose one or the other.

Pursue God and turn from immorality. Cease living a life of irreverent normalcy consumed with compromise, and instead, reach a radical resolve. Observe the Oracle. Adopt a paradigm shift mentality in fearing the Lord relentlessly, and discover the favor of God!

ENDNOTES

1   Oracle [Def. 5]. (n.d.). Dictionary Online. Retrieved February 22, 2016, from http://www.dictionary.com/browse/oracle.

2   *Bruce Almighty*. Dir. Tom Shadyac. Universal Studios, 2003. Film.

3   Blessing [Def. 3,4]. (n.d.). Dictionary Online. Retrieved February 24, 2016, from http://www.dictionary.com/browse/blessing.

4   Curse [Def. 1,6]. (n.d.). Dictionary Online. Retrieved February 24, 2016, from http://www.dictionary.com/browse/curse.

5   Os Guinness, *The Call*. Nashville, TN. W Publishing Group, a Division of Thomas Nelson, Inc. 1998, 2003), 25.

6   *New International Version*. Bible Gateway. Web. Retrieved on 7 July 2015.

7   Louis Pasteur. The History Learning Site. Retrieved on 7 July 2015.

8   A.W. Tozer, *The Root of the Righteous* (Harrisburg, PA: Christian Publications, 1955), 137.

Printed in the United States
By Bookmasters